THE HOME DECORATOR SERIES

CHAIRS
CUSHIONS
AND COVERINGS

THE HOME DECORATOR SERIES

CHAIRS CUSHIONS AND COVERINGS

LORRIE MACK

CONRAN OCTOPUS

First published in 1986 by
Conran Octopus Limited
28-32 Shelton Street
London WC2 9PH

Copyright © Conran Octopus Limited 1986

Consultant Editor Hilary More
House Editor Sarah Bevan
Designer Alan Marshall
Picture research Nadine Bazar
Production Jill Embleton

ISBN 1 85029 054 7

Typeset by SX Composing Ltd

Printed and bound in Spain

CONTENTS

SEDUCTIVE SEATING

We look to our homes to provide, above all, a place where we can relax and feel completely comfortable, and the right seating will go a long way toward bringing this about. That doesn't just mean choosing an appropriately-designed chair: your perfect seating may involve generous piles of cushions, or seat pads tailor-made for your own chairs, with covers in fabrics that camouflage dirty marks. Our recognition of the importance of seating in our homes is reflected in the fact that we ask so many things from this single element.

Firstly, we expect it, like all items of domestic furnishing, to look attractive – to complement our rooms and our personalities and to express our ideas of taste and suitability. When you are searching for a chair or sofa, however strongly you feel about the practicality of a potential purchase, you will probably be drawn initially by the look of the thing.

At the same time, we demand that our seating supports us comfortably, and for extended periods, in a position for which the human body was never designed – with the behind (and usually the back) held in place at an appropriate height for the legs to hang down and the feet to touch the floor.

In addition to these obvious functions, most items of seating in our homes finish up being pressed into service in a wide variety of unsuitable ways: as step-ladders, trampolines, sleeping places for pets, clothes stands, foot-rests, workbenches, and most commonly, repositories for possessions we intend to put away at a more convenient time.

The degree to which your seating fulfils all these requirements will depend on the amount of thought, energy and imagination you are prepared to invest. Few of us can throw away what we don't like and begin again with unlimited resources, so first of all try to improve what you already have by camouflaging comfortable but ugly pieces and padding pretty but unyielding ones. Before you set out to buy anything new, arm yourself with a knowledge of what's available in the shops and consider your individual requirements carefully.

The relaxed, convivial atmosphere of a private club has been recreated in this stylish room by replacing the sometimes inflexible three-piece suite with an unusual assortment of invitingly oversized 1920s armchairs.

YOUR NEEDS

Whether you are furnishing your rooms from scratch, adding individual pieces as a result of an increase in the size of your home, your household or your income, or replacing worn and broken items, you will soon become aware that seating of all kinds represents a considerable financial outlay. If you bought your last sofa or chair a long time ago, you may even become convinced that the cost of these items has risen disproportionately, but with a few exceptions (anything containing oil-based products like foam or plastic has increased in price particularly sharply), furniture hasn't been hit by inflation harder than anything else. Even so, seating constitutes a major investment, which makes it particularly important that you should choose wisely.

Cost

Cost is inevitably going to be a major influence on your final choice, but before you start comparing styles and prices, make sure you have a clear idea of your seating needs. The dictum that you should always buy the very best you can afford is often repeated, and with excellent reason – it is unswervingly true that higher quality means a piece of furniture will wear better and keep its good looks longer. But longevity may not be one of the features you require, particularly if you demand frequent changes in your surroundings; a Victorian-style Chesterfield crafted to such a superb standard that it will last a lifetime is not a prudent purchase if you know that in the next few years you are likely to be seized with the desire to re-do the living room in, for example, an Art Deco style.

It's also true that the quality of an item that will not be subject to heavy wear (perhaps because it will be used only in a bedroom or a very formal dining room, or when it is intended only for guest seating in a small household) need not necessarily be as high as that of one constantly in use. Similarly, it would be inappropriate to furnish a home with seating made of precious materials that are vulnerable to surface damage, if it runs a serious risk of destruction by marauding small children and pets.

When you've decided roughly what you want to pay, you

Try to find a workable balance between the quality and practicality you require from a potential furnishing purchase and the amount you can afford to pay for it.

Left: Sturdy beech chairs with woven seats may not be passed on to your grandchildren, but they will give years of faithful service and good looks at a reasonable price.

Below: The very finest quality: a Le Corbusier design interpreted in fresh, bright colours. Many cheaper versions borrow its revolutionary principle of putting the frame on the outside.

may have to use a great deal of self-discipline to stick to this figure – furniture shops are beguiling places in which you may be tempted by a persuasive salesman or an extravagant display to commit yourself to a greater expenditure than you originally intended.

Style

When you come to choose the style of your seating, your first considerations will probably be the period of the rest of the furnishings and, to a certain extent, of your home itself. Widely different styles in both can be combined very effectively, but it takes a sure eye for design and considerable confidence, so if you feel nervous, don't stray too far from the look of the things you already own. On the whole, low modern styles tend to make the smaller, boxier rooms of new properties look bigger and higher, while large-scale traditional pieces were designed to set off the generous proportions of older properties.

If you are furnishing your first home, you may be unsure of the seating style you want – or even of the general atmosphere in which you would be happy. If this is the case, don't agonize about it too much. Leaf slowly through as many design books and magazines as you can gather, and you will find that before long certain kinds of rooms consistently catch your eye – cool, modern ones, subtly-hued traditional ones, exotic oriental ones or jazzy brightly-coloured ones. Make a note of the furnishing characteristics that turn up repeatedly in the rooms you admire, and take your cue from these.

Comfort

Whatever overall style you pick, the overriding requirement for the selection of any item should be the degree of comfort it offers. In recent years, the science of ergonomics – the relationship between the human body and its immediate environment in the form of furniture, tools, accessories and machines – has influenced the design of furniture, and particularly of chairs intended for office use. The best of these are now highly adjustable to the individual user and constructed to offer maximum support whether you lean back

or forward or sit in a fairly upright position.

Domestic seating, unfortunately, has lagged behind, but there are various pointers to look for in a comfortable chair. The proportions of a chair or sofa – the height of its seat from the floor, the height of its back, the width and depth of its seat – are vitally important, so be sure to take these into account. Generally speaking, a comfortable chair will provide good support for the back and the full length of the thighs, and have a seat that falls approximately at knee height. Think of the people who will be sitting on your purchase: a household that includes several sprawling, oversized teenagers will not be well served by delicate chairs designed for an eighteenth-century drawing room.

Examine closely any seating you find particularly comfortable and try to determine what it is that gives the piece this special feeling so that you can attempt to choose a new article with the same characteristics. Try out all prospective buys, but bear in mind that they will be tested fully only after they are in your home and occupied for hours on end, so don't depend on a shop trial as your only guideline.

If you fall in love with an item of seating that does not meet your particular requirements for comfort, you are justified in giving it house room only if you are very sure it won't be using up money or space that would be better invested in a more user-friendly article.

Size and position

The last important need to consider is the simplest to establish if not always the simplest to cope with – the right dimensions for each item required. When you go to a shop, take with you the measurements of your room and of any existing pieces. When you spot something you like, measure it as well to find out if it will fit into the space you have in mind, leaving enough surrounding space so it can be used without crowding its occupant, its neighbours, or any passing traffic.

Next, decide what degree of flexibility in arrangement you want – it may be that your chosen item will fit into your room in only one place, thus making it impossible to re-arrange your furniture from time to time. Try not to leave yourself without this option, especially if you're moving into a new home, since it is often not until you have lived with a room for a while that you are able to get a feeling of how it should best be organized – which spots are most vulnerable to draughts for example, or which areas command the best view from the window. Traffic paths take time to become established as well, and family members moving to and from the telephone, dining room or television will not appreciate having to run an obstacle course through a forest of easy chairs.

Remember, too, to allow space for a table of some kind near each easy chair or sofa. The lack of a convenient surface will result in, at best, plates and glasses balanced uncomfortably on knees or padded arms, and, at worst, an assortment of red wine and coffee stains on the carpet.

Special needs

Many children find the idea of their own scaled-down furniture enchanting, and you will find a wide variety of pint-sized items at every price range. Moulded plastic seats, often in animal shapes, are cheap and fun and they can readily be discarded when the child outgrows them. Look, too, for convertible designs such as a baby's high chair that adapts to become a small table and chair for a toddler. If you are attracted to costly antique children's furniture such as tiny Lloyd loom chairs, make sure you appreciate their dainty proportions enough to justify their presence in your home even after the little ones have grown up.

The most important aspect of children's furniture is safety – make sure every item is strong enough to withstand rough handling and stable enough not to collapse when stood or climbed on. In the case of folding pieces, make extra sure that they cannot snap shut on tiny fingers.

Safety is also a key factor in furnishing a room that will be used by elderly people. Try to provide chairs with a high seat (knee level is definitely preferable in this case) and firm back support. Sturdy arms, especially if they are the right width to provide a good grip, are useful for leverage, and straight legs are safer than those that splay outwards, which could trip partially-sighted people or those unsteady on their feet.

Many older people appreciate a footstool and this is, in any case, a useful piece of furniture that can serve as an extra seat or as a temporary storage place for books and magazines.

Household members who suffer from chronic back pain will also have specific seating requirements, but these will differ according to the location and nature of the complaint, so it's best for them to follow specialist advice when it comes to their seating arrangements.

Secondhand seating

There are two main reasons for buying furniture secondhand – because you love it or because you're short of money. It's true that many pieces are no more expensive – and some even less so – than their modern relations, and the quality is often vastly superior. Secondhand kitchen or dining chairs can

Far left: Many items of secondhand furniture have a very individual charm that is hard to find in modern, mass-produced pieces. This delightful cane armchair provides a comfortable place for reading or sewing in a bedroom where the emphasis is on tradition.

Left: When the effect you want is one of air and space, choose furniture made from clear plastic, which is visually light as well as easy to move around.

sometimes be bargains, but go carefully if you plan to save pennies by buying a chair or sofa in need of re-upholstering. If done professionally, this is often a very expensive service that could cost you more than the price of a similar article in the shops. Upholstery is certainly possible for the amateur to learn, but, depending on the degree of deterioration in the item you have bought, it can be complex, time-consuming and heavy work that should not be undertaken by the faint-hearted. Upholstered dining chairs, however, can be easily transformed by the replacement of the old covers on the seat, back and arms with new ones in fabrics of your own choosing (pages 64-71). Colourful and unusual cushions (pages 22-39) will rejuvenate any plain hard chair; and for an irredeemably worn or faded sofa, a throw-over, no-sew cover could provide the answer (pages 72-5).

Final choice

Learn to accept that the piece you end up with will probably be, to some extent, a compromise between what you adore, what you need and what is available in your price range. It would be very foolish indeed to buy any item of furniture in haste, simply because doing without it is inconvenient – take time, look around, think about it, even if you have to manage with a makeshift substitute for a while.

On the other hand, be realistic: sitting on orange boxes for years while you wait for the perfect dining chair to present itself is just as daft. If you weigh up your needs carefully, do some background reading, make a few crucial decisions on style, colour and layout, and make a reasonable effort to find out what is available in the shops, your purchase has a much better chance of being the right one.

CUSHIONS

One of the earliest forms of furnishing employed by man, cushions were for centuries the only thing coming between him and the stone or wooden seats that provided him with something to sit on. Even now, a pile of downy cushions improves even the most highly padded piece of furniture and gives a welcoming, friendly look to any room.

If you are short on cash or sewing skills, two pieces of fabric simply stitched together will make a perfectly serviceable cover, but for the slightly more ambitious, there is no end to the styles and effects that can be created: square, round or fancy designs; flat shapes, those with generous welts, or fat, cylindrical bolsters; trimming of every description – piping, borders, frills or pleats.

Use bright cushions to relieve large areas of neutral colour, or layer softly-hued ones to build up a subtle pattern-on-pattern effect. Choose fabrics that match your other furnishings if you like a controlled, co-ordinated look, or search out pretty, single specimens if yours is a more relaxed style.

Make cushions work for you by adding them to chests, trunks, window ledges and blanket boxes to make extra seating. Pile them on a divan to disguise the sleeping area in a bedsitter, but be careful to choose pads of an appropriate size, and be generous with them, since a few tiny cushions strung along the back of a bed will only look untidy.

Invest in two or three huge floor cushions to expand the entertaining facilities in a teenager's bedroom or to supplement the existing seating when the whole family comes to call. Try to avoid choosing floor cushions as your only seating however; undeniably economical, this arrangement is almost always uncomfortable for elderly people or those with any physical disability, so unless you are very sure that everyone you entertain is young and spry enough to enjoy this very casual style, make some effort to adapt your floor cushions for wider use. You could do this by adding back cushions and putting them both on a raised plinth.

A perfect setting for sun-
drenched breakfasts. The
severe lines of this slatted wood
bench (and its hard surface) have
been relieved by a cheerful bank
of stripey cushions in a variety of
bold colours and patterns.

Above: Use cushions to gain extra seating when you entertain a crowd. There are so many piled on this trunk that several could be pressed into service as floor cushions, perhaps for children.

Right: Built-in benches often make the best use of dining space, but usually at the expense of comfort. Few would complain about this arrangement, however, made luxurious by adding cushions.

Left: The occupant of this small but well-planned flat has catered for all social eventualities: one or two guests are accommodated on the sofa and chair, while larger numbers spill over on to the cushion-covered mattresses, which also provide a bed for overnight visitors.

Below: The rough, natural surfaces and long, low, simple lines of this striking modern house make a perfect background against which to display the rich colours and intricate patterns of primitive textiles – on the walls, on the divan and, most dramatically, on the huge cushions.

CUSHION CONSTRUCTION

Fillings, clockwise from left: foam, in chips and as solid block; synthetic wadding; kapok; Polyester filling; curled feathers; polystyrene granules.

To be (and to remain) practical as well as pretty, your cushions should have a soft, resilient filling, a casing to prevent this filling from escaping and to provide a smooth surface, and an outer cover that has been neatly and accurately sewn using techniques appropriate to the type of cushion you want.

Fillings

Most cushion pads contain one of the following types of filling:
FEATHERS One of the most traditional and widely-used fillings – and certainly the most expensive – feathers (or more luxurious still, feathers and down) will repay their initial cost by providing soft and inviting cushions that need only a gentle shake to regain their original shape after use.

Many department stores carry a large range of feather pads in the most commonly required sizes and shapes (square, rectangular, round) so for simple cushions without welts you should have no trouble finding one to suit your purpose. If you want to make your own, you can use the feathers from old cushions (or pillows) in shapes that are no longer wanted (transfer the filling into its new case out of doors on a still day). but remember that feathers have a finite existence, so you'll be disappointed if you try to recycle very old, droopy cushions that have lost all their resilience. When choosing the new casing, it's particularly important that you look for special, closely woven material – downproof cambric or ticking – that will not allow the feathers to leak out.
KAPOK Another old-fashioned stuffing material, kapok is a vegetable fibre (it looks much like raw cotton) that surrounds the seeds of a tropical tree. Kapok pads have a similar look and feel to feather ones, but they cannot be washed and they will become thin and lumpy much more quickly. Although it is still available, this filling has largely been replaced by longer-lasting man-made materials.
POLYESTER FILLING is a very efficient man-made alternative to kapok. It has the advantages of being completely washable and also hypo-allergenic.
FOAM is used in two forms for filling cushions: solid blocks, or shredded into tiny chips. Cushions made from both types are completely washable, and therefore particularly suitable for use outside on garden furniture or in children's rooms.

Use foam blocks cut to size for awkwardly-shaped squab cushions, or for inexpensive large cushions shaped to fit the seat of a sofa or chair (pages 50-1). Solid foam is sold in several densities to suit different purposes, so tell the assistant what you want it for and ask for advice.

Foam chips are widely available and constitute one of the cheapest fillings possible, making them the most common choice for floor cushions. The main disadvantage of this material is its bumpy uneven texture that shows through all but the thickest fabric.

You may feel tempted to omit the inner casing of a foam cushion, especially when you're using a solid block filling, but foam tends to crumble into small particles in use, and the casing is particularly important because it contains these bits.
SYNTHETIC WADDING is made from man-made fibres like Polyester, bonded together to make a useful soft-furnishing material that is extremely light, completely washable and available in several weights (thicknesses): ask for it under the trade names of Polyester, Courtelle or Dacron.
POLYSTYRENE GRANULES are most commonly used to stuff large floor cushions and 'bean bags'. They move around within the cushion so that it moulds itself to the shape of the sitter, provided the cushion is not over-stuffed.

Cutting the cover

First, think about the size of your finished cushion and choose an appropriate fabric. Floor cushions, for example, may be subject to heavy wear, so cover them in a fabric that will be suitable. Fabric widths can range from 90cm (36in.) to 150cm (60in.), depending on whether it is intended for dressmaking or furnishing, so remember to take width into account when estimating the amount you need. Plain or small-patterned fabrics can generally be used most economically, because the cover pieces can be cut out side by side. Large patterns will require more fabric, since you should centre the main motif on each cushion.

Square and rectangular cushion covers should be cut on the straight grain of the fabric. To do this, either cut into the

fabric (through the selvedge if necessary) and tear it across the width; or pull one weft thread and cut along the gap.

If you find that your fabric is printed inaccurately – with the design running at an angle to, rather than along, the straight of grain – follow the pattern rather than the weave: on a small area like a cushion irregularities would be very obvious.

Generally speaking, cut your two cover pieces to the same size as your pad: by the time you have sewn the cover up, deducting a seam allowance of 1.5cm (⅝in.) all round, you will have a cover slightly smaller than the pad and therefore a firm, plump cushion. If your pad is firmly stuffed already, or if you are making cushions with welts, allow extra fabric for the seam allowances before you cut the cover pieces out. Unless otherwise stated, the seam allowance on all the projects in this book is the standard 1.5cm (⅝in.).

Hints on making up

Unless you are very experienced in sewing, you will get the best results if you pin each seam, then tack it in place temporarily before stitching it neatly with a sewing-machine or by hand. Remove all tacking stitches when the cushion is finished. When you are more confident you will find pinning is sufficient in most cases to hold the fabric before sewing it.

To neaten seams, trim the seam allowances to 1cm (⅜in.), then overstitch all the edges together by hand or machine, and perhaps using a zigzag stitch if your machine has a swing needle. Frilled or piped cushions (pages 22-3 and 24-7), or any with several layers of fabric caught into one seam, may need neatening in this way. If you want a seam to lie flat, for example when making a bolster cushion (pages 34-5), zigzag each raw edge separately, then press the seam open.

Make French seams where extra strength is required – for example on floor cushions, where the seams are put under strain – or when raw edges would look better enclosed, as on a single frill (page 22). With wrong sides facing and raw edges matching, stitch a 6mm (¼in.) seam. Turn the seam back on itself so the right sides of fabric are facing. Stitch another seam 1cm (⅜in.) from the seamed edge.

You will get a neater finish on all your work if you press it carefully at each stage.

FASTENINGS

The simplest fastening method, and one that will ensure a neat finish, is a line of slipstitching along the cushion's edge. Pin, tack and stitch your two pieces of fabric with right sides facing along three sides and round all four corners; stitch in for about 5cm (2in.) on the fourth side, leaving a central opening. Turn the cover to the right side, push out the corners and press, turning in the edges of the opening in line with the remainder of the seam. Insert your cushion pad or stuffing and slipstitch closed.

Zip fasteners

The most common type of fastening is a zip. Choose a light- to medium-weight zip in a colour that co-ordinates with your fabric, 8cm (3in.) shorter than the side into which it will be inserted. Stitch it into place using the zipper foot on your machine, or by hand using small even backstitches. For a zip across the back of a cushion, remember to cut the back cover piece larger than the front by 3cm (1 1/4in.), then cut it in half. Insert the zip centrally or low down near an edge.

Touch-and-close spots

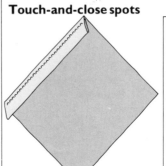

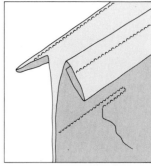

1. Pin and stitch a 1.5cm (⅝in.) hem along matching edges of both pieces of fabric. Fold hem over again for 1.5cm (⅝in.) and press.

2. With right sides facing, stitch pieces together alongside hem for 4cm (1 1/2in.) in from both sides, leaving a central opening for fastenings.

Slipstitching

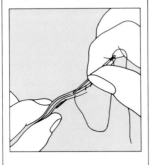

1. Fasten thread inside one folded edge. Take needle through opposite fold for 3mm (⅛in.). Take the needle across opening and repeat.

Non-fastening vent

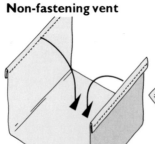

1. Cut fabric twice as long as the cover, plus 8cm (3in.). Add 3cm (1 1/4in.) to width for seams. Stitch a 1cm (⅜in.) double hem on short edges.

2. Right sides together, fold the hemmed ends of the fabric so they overlap in the middle by 4cm (1 1/2in.). Stitch side seams. Turn to right side.

Inserting zip in seam

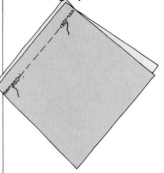

1. Right sides facing, pin and tack the two pieces of fabric together along one edge only. Stitch in from both ends for 4cm (1 1/2in.) leaving opening.

Press or touch-and-close fasteners

For press fasteners or light-weight touch-and-close spots or strips, add an extra 3cm (1 1/4in.) seam allowance to one dimension when you cut out the fabric. This allows for a double hem on to which the fasteners can be stitched.

Positioning your fastening

If your cushion has a large motif on it, or if the pattern runs in one direction only, the fastening should be inserted in the side that runs along the base of the design.

Pretty alternatives

For a very pretty effect, leave one side of the cushion open, slipstitch a hem along each edge, then attach lengths of ribbon at corresponding positions and tie your cover closed. You could even do this all round the cushion, without stitching any of the seams at all. For a laced effect, make two rows of reinforced holes using an eyelet kit (page 54), then thread cord or ribbon through and tie.

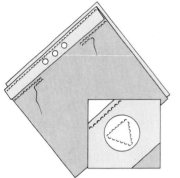
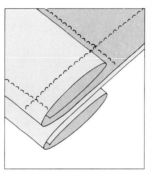

3. Using a triangular pattern of stitching, anchor touch-and-close spots through single hem; or handstitch press fasteners in position.

4. With right sides facing, stitch remaining three sides of cover together, catching down the pressed double hems with the stitching at each side.

Inserting zip across back

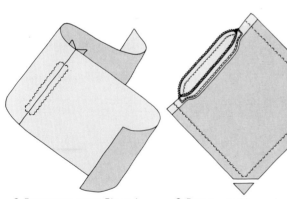

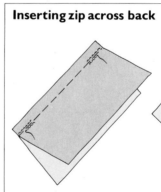

2. Press seam open. Pin and tack zip face down on wrong side of seam with the teeth over the tacked section of seam. Stitch from right side.

3. Remove tacking and open zip. With right sides facing, stitch remaining three edges of cushion cover. Turn cover to right side through zip.

1. Right sides facing, pin and tack back pieces together. Stitch in for 4cm (1 1/2in.) from each edge, leaving a central opening.

2. Press seam open. Pin and tack zip, right side down, centrally over tacked opening in seam. Stitch in place from right side. Complete cover.

FRILLS

One of the quickest and easiest ways to trim any type of cushion is with a frill, plain or pleated, in a fabric that matches or contrasts with the cover. Try gathering your frill at the corners only, or layer several frills of different widths and fabrics into one seam; you could also pipe the front cover piece as well (pages 24-7). Frills create an instant impression of extravagance, and you could exploit this by stitching several of them on to a cover piece in concentric circles, working from the outer edge inwards.

Depending on the degree of fullness you want, cut the fabric for the frill 1½-2 times the perimeter of the cushion. With a pleated frill, the width of each pleat should divide equally into the sides of the cushion, with one extra pleat at each corner. Multiply the width of the pleat by three, then multiply by the number of pleats: cut a strip of fabric to this length, on the straight of grain.

To make inverted pleats, as shown in our picture, make sure you have an even number of pleats down each side, then fold alternate pleats towards the previous one.

Cushions with frills

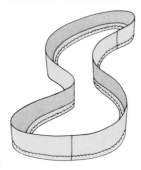

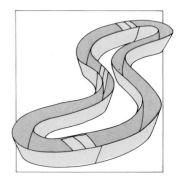

1. For single frill, cut fabric on straight of grain and join strips with French seams. Stitch a 1cm (⅜in.) double hem along one edge.

2. For double frill, join bias fabric strips, right sides facing, using plain seams. Press seams open. Fold lengthwise, wrong sides together.

Pleated frills

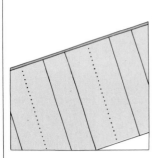

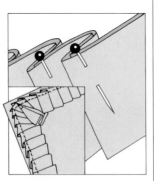

1. Make up frill (double or single) as before. Mark knife pleats indicating placement and fold lines. (Broken lines are inner fold lines.)

2. Fold fabric to form pleats. Pin, tack along both edges, and press. Attach to cover piece: there will be two pleats at each corner. Stitch and complete.

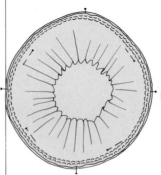

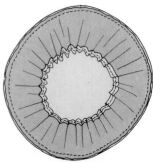

4. Match sections of frill with markings on cover piece, right sides together (5. shows single frill). Ease gathers to fit, and pin in position.

5. Stitch frill to cover piece, anchoring the gathers in place. Right sides facing, stitch on remaining piece and complete the cover.

Use decorative borders to give your cushions a distinctive style – soft frills for a purely feminine effect (right) or neat pleats for a crisp, country feeling (below right).

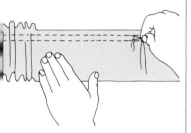

3. Mark the edge of one cover piece and the frill into sections. Run two rows of gathering stitches along each section of the frill. Pull up gathers.

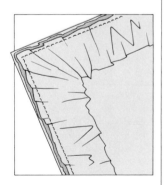

6. On a square cushion, divide frill into four sections. Pull up gathers and match sections to sides. Allow extra gathers at corners. Stitch and complete.

PIPING

Piped cushions are popular, simple and endlessly variable. Piping can be fat, thin or even flat (join strips as below, press in half lengthwise, and attach to your cover piece without any cord); it can be gathered or plain. You can even layer rows of piping one on top of another, using different colours. If you want the effect of piping without the effort, stitch a length of braid or twisted cord around the edges of your finished cushion cover.

Covered piping cord not only gives a professional finish to cushion seams, it also makes them stronger – an important factor on seat and floor cushions. The cord itself is available in a wide range of sizes from 00 to 6, so choose the one most suitable for the weight and content of your fabric: for most cottons nos. 3 or 4 would work well, but if you are unsure take along a piece of your fabric when you buy your cord, and ask for advice. Most piping cord is pre-shrunk, and this is important since cord that shrinks more than its covering fabric will cause your piping to pucker the seams. Unless you are certain this pre-shrinking has been done, simmer the cord

Corded cushions

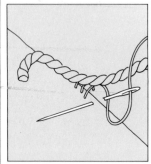

1. Leave a small opening centrally in cover seam. Stitch cord along seam line, picking up a few threads across seam and through base of cord.

2. At the opening, tuck the cord ends into the seam so they overlap inside the cover. Stitch cords together, then the opening round them.

Simple piping

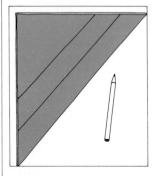

1. Fold fabric diagonally so selvedge lies parallel with weft threads. Working from fold, mark strips of required width. Cut out strips.

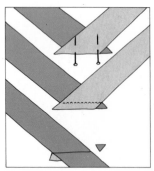

2. Right sides facing, stitch strips together along straight grain taking 6mm (¼in.) seam allowance. Trim ends. Press seams open.

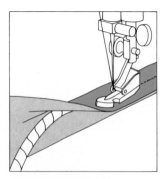

3. With wrong sides facing, fold finished strip in half lengthwise around piping cord. Stitch alongside cord, using piping foot attachment.

4. On square cover, stitch piping to right side of one piece, raw edges together. At corners, snip into piping fabric up to stitching.

Those not particularly adept at needlework can add an attractive trim to their cushions by stitching on a length of ready-made cord, which is available in plain colours or with several different colours twisted together.

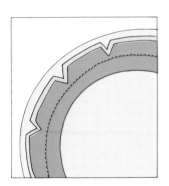

5. On round cover, snip into piping fabric at 2.5cm (1 in.) intervals before placing round cover piece. With raw edges matching, pin, tack and stitch.

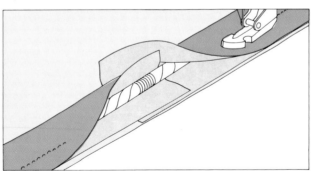

6. To join the cord, trim both cord ends and butt them firmly together. Bind over the join several times with strong sewing thread.

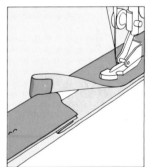

7. To join fabric, trim so one edge overlaps the other by 2cm (¾in.). Turn under 1cm (⅜in.) and place over raw edge. Complete stitching.

for three minutes, then dry flat before you start to assemble your piping.

Fabric for piping is always cut on the bias so it has enough 'give' to go round the cushion. Cut strips wide enough to cover the cord, adding 3cm (1¼in.) for seam allowances. Always join the strips together on the straight of grain to prevent the seams from stretching out of shape. Stitch the fabric round the cord using the piping or zipper foot on your machine, and stitch very close to the cord. For gathered piping, your strip of fabric will need to be 1½-2 times the length of the cord, and in this case do not stitch too close to the cord – the fabric will not pull up easily to form the gathers.

If you want a much plumper border round your cushion, use rolled up synthetic wadding instead of piping cord. Cut your fabric strips on the bias as before, but wider.

For a fastening, either insert a zip across one cover piece before you attach the piping; or stitch the piping to one cover piece first, then insert a zip or other fastening into a seam before joining the cover pieces together.

Gathered piping cord

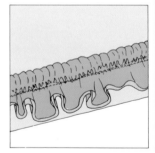

1. Place cord inside fabric. Stitch for 20cm (8in.). Raise foot leaving needle in fabric. Gently pull cord through fabric to gather; repeat.

2. Position the gathered cord round the cover – whether square or round – making sure gathers look even. Join ends of cord and fabric as on page 25.

Fat piping

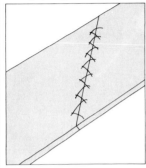 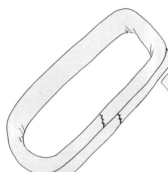 

1. Cut several lengths of medium-weight wadding 7cm (3in.) wide. Cut ends diagonally; butt ends and join with herringbone stitch.

2. Join ends as before to form a circle. Roll up the wadding to make a sausage-shaped ring, and hold in place temporarily with pins.

3. Wrong sides together, fold fabric in half round wadding. Stitch, removing pins as you go. Position and stitch piping to cover as on pages 24-5.

How to make continuous piping fabric

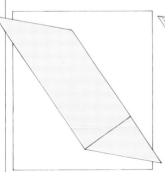 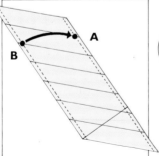 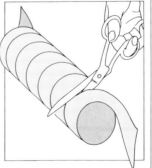

1. Cut a rectangle of fabric 25 × 50cm (10 × 20in.). Fold down one corner at right angles. Cut off triangle and stitch to opposite end.

2. On right side and using tailor's chalk, mark out strips parallel to bias edge. Mark A and B as shown, 1cm (⅜in.) from outer edges.

3. Right sides facing, place A to B. Stitch edges together to make a tube. Turn to right side. Cut out one long piping strip following marked lines.

SIMPLE BORDERS

These cushions have the plainest, perhaps the most elegant border of all, a simple 'flange' of about 6cm (2½in.) wide. In our picture we show cushions with single and double borders, with colours mixed and matched, but you could be more inventive in your combinations: for a bold, graphic look, cut each cover piece in four sections, two in each of two colours, and stitch together in a chequerboard pattern before you assemble the cover. You could line the borders of a double-bordered cushion with contrasting or co-ordinating fabric; or use a border print – a scarf or handkerchief.

To make a single border, add twice the width of your border plus seam allowances to each dimension of your cushion pad, and cut your cover pieces to this size. For a double flange you will need to add four times the width of the border, plus seam allowance.

A single bordered cushion can simply be slipstitched closed. Zips or press fasteners should be inserted across one cover piece before you make the cushion up: add extra seam allowances to one dimension of one cover piece.

Cushions with double borders

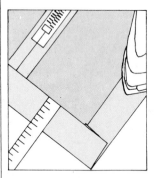 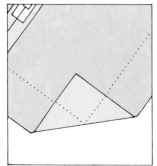 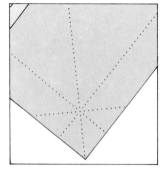 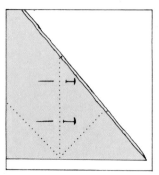

1. Lay back section flat, wrong side up. Fold in a border of the required width plus seam allowance all round and press. Repeat for other piece.

2. Open out. Fold in each corner point until pressed lines on corner align with those along edges of cover. Press this diagonal fold.

3. Open out corner again. Then, with wrong sides facing, fold cover in half diagonally through corner, matching fabric edges carefully. Press.

4. Right sides facing, fold in half along bias and stitch across corner along fold line now at right angles. Trim seam to 6mm (¼in.) and press open.

Single borders

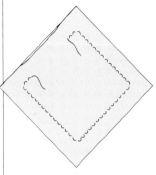

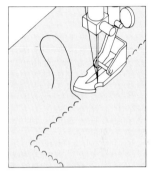

1. Right sides facing, stitch squares together, leaving gap for filling. Turn to right side. Stitch round cover at chosen width leaving same opening.

2. Insert filling through both openings. Stitch across inner opening, matching up with previous stitching using piping foot attachment.

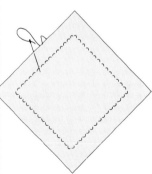

3. Turn in open edges in line with the remainder of the outer seamed edge. Slipstitch the two folded edges together to close.

4. Insert any fastening across one cover piece before you begin. Open zip, if using. Stitch cover together, turn to right side and stitch round pad.

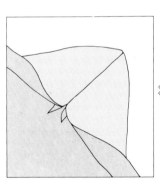

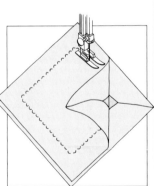

5. Turn corner through to right side and press resulting mitre. Repeat these steps on remaining corners of both top and bottom cover pieces.

6. Wrong sides facing, and matching mitred corners together, stitch cover pieces together at required border distance from outer edge.

CUSHIONS WITH WELTS

Cushions with narrow welts come into their own when a geometric, box-like shape is required, or when you want some degree of additional thickness in a throw cushion. (More substantial, welted seat cushions are described on pages 50-1.) You could use a contrasting colour or pattern for the welts, or gather the top and bottom cover pieces of a round cushion as if it were the end of a bolster (page 34): give it a plain, not gathered, welt. Welted throw cushions are usually filled with pads of the same shape, or you could use slabs of foam.

Cut the welt pieces on the straight of grain, adding seam allowances. For a square or rectangular shape, or any cushions with corners, cut the welt in as many sections as sides and match the seams to the corners. Once you have attached your welt to one cover piece, insert a zip or press fasteners before attaching the other cover piece; or insert a fastening across the latter.

For a gathered welt, cut your strip of fabric 1½-2 times longer than the cushion's perimeter.

Welts for square cushions

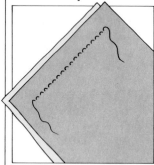 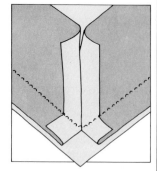

1. Right sides facing, stitch welt pieces into a ring, leaving 1.5cm (⅝in.) unstitched at either end of each seam. Press open.

2. Right sides facing, stitch welt to one cover piece. At corners seams will split open: stitch across top to provide sharp corners. Complete cover.

Welts for round cushions

 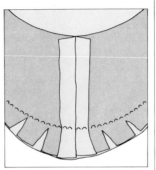

1. Right sides facing, join welt pieces together across their full width. Stitch into a ring long enough to go round cushion. Press seams open.

2. Snip into seam allowance of both edges of welt at 2.5cm (1 in.) intervals. Right sides facing, stitch welt to one cover piece, then the other.

Gathered welt for a square cushion

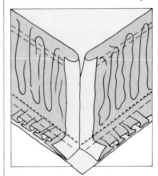 

1. Join and gather welt as described opposite and below. Stitch to cover pieces, splitting open seams at corners. Leave an opening.

2. Turn cover to right side. Insert cushion pad. Turn in edges of opening in line with seam and slipstitch together to close.

Gathered welt for a round cushion

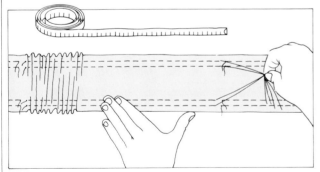 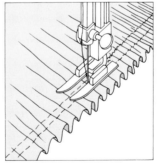 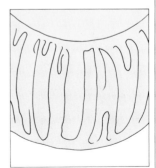

1. Stitch welt strips together as above. Divide both welt and cover pieces into sections, as for frills (page 22). On each section, work two rows of gathering stitches along each edge of welt. Pull up equally, and match to sections on cover piece. Adjust gathers, distributing evenly along welt.

2. Stitch over gathers along both edges to anchor fullness in place before attaching welt to cover: follow inner rows of gathering stitches.

3. Right sides facing, stitch gathered welt to round cover pieces, leaving an opening. Turn to right side. Insert pad; slipstitch opening.

CORNER VARIATIONS

Add stylish detailing to your cushions by subtly altering the shape of their corners.

Simplest of all are corners gathered as described below: sew together your two cover pieces, right sides facing and inserting an appropriate fastening, then gather up each corner. For a gentler curve, illustrated right, gather each corner of fabric before you begin to make up the cushion. Experiment on a piece of spare fabric until you get the degree of fullness you want, measure this, then make sure you gather all the corners by the same amount. Pipe one cover piece for a really sophisticated look, before you add a fastening and complete the cover.

Mock welts, with their softly curving edges, can be achieved by stitching across the corners at right angles to the seam. Complete your cover first, cutting your cover pieces to the size of the top of the pad plus half the depth of the border plus seam allowances. You could use this sort of cover for shallow pads or pieces of foam, as opposite, but also for cushions of any proportion.

Gathered corners

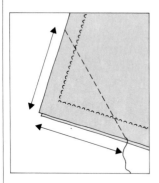

1. Make up cushion cover. Mark two points, each one 3cm (1¼in.) along the side seam from one corner. Gather across the corner by hand.

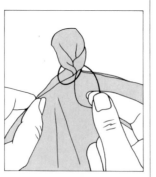

2. Pull up stitches, then wind cotton tightly and repeatedly around gathered-up corner. Fasten off. Repeat at other corners. Complete cover.

Piped and gathered cushions

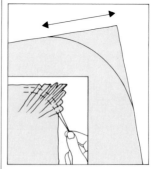

1. Mark two points on each edge of fabric, 6cm (2½in.) from a corner. Join points in a curve. Work two rows of gathering stitches and pull up.

2. Repeat on all eight corners, and trim. Make up piping to right length and stitch in place; snip up to stitching at corners. Complete cover.

Far left: Cushions with softly-gathered corners are easy to make and they will give a lovely, informal feeling to your room; to show them to best advantage, provide a large enough pad to give a plump, inviting shape.

Left: Use the mock gusset technique to make simple geometric cushions. Here, square shapes in ice-cream colours are stacked in a neat, formal pile.

Mock welts

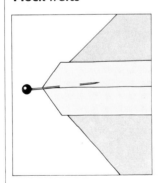

1. Make up cushion cover. Pull cover pieces apart at each corner so you can centre one seam flat on top of the one along next edge. Pin in place.

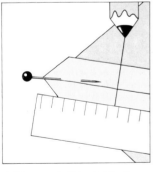

2. Measure half the finished depth of 'gusset' along seam and mark at right angles to seam. Stitch across corner along marked line.

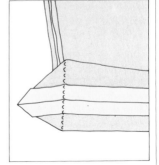

3. Repeat for other three corners. Without trimming off corner points, press mock welts and turn cover to right side. Insert pad or filling.

BOLSTERS

Cylindrical cushions traditionally found along the backs of beds, couches and *chaise-longues*, bolsters are still in common use in some countries like France, and, as in our picture, are often used to support a row of throw cushions of all shapes and sizes. They are commonly of a length to fit across a bed, either double or single, and can be invaluable for increasing the seating flexibility of a divan; but their uses can be much more varied than that. Small ones make good neck pillows, whether for watching television or for making a long car journey a little more comfortable; bolsters in a slightly larger size might also be useful in the back seat of a car, particularly if you have disabled or elderly passengers. In the house, children or teenagers who are really comfortable only when they are sprawled on the floor might appreciate a large bolster, particularly if it was so long it could be curled round itself, tied in a knot, or coiled into a bucket seat. Such a bolster could be as long as 10 metres (11 yards), with a diameter of 20-25cm (8-10in.), depending on the width of your fabric. Use heavy cotton, perhaps ticking, and cut it in half length-

A bolster cushion

1. To make template for end circles, cut a square of paper slightly larger than required circle. Fold paper accurately into quarters.

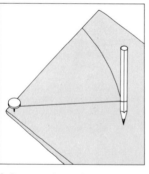

2. Fasten a piece of string into folded corner with a drawing pin. Tie to a pencil so its length is the radius of required circle. Draw an arc and cut out.

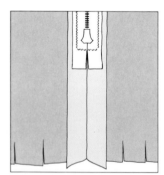

3. Right sides facing, stitch main fabric into a cylinder, leaving central tacked section. Insert zip. Cut notches in both ends 2.5cm (1 in.) apart.

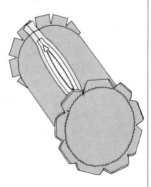

4. Adding seam allowance to template, cut two end circles. Notch as before. Open zip. Right sides facing, stitch to cover. Turn to right side.

The two full-sized divans in this pretty bedsitter are transformed into attractive and comfortable sofas by the clever use of fat bolsters, padded backs and elegant flanged cushions (pages 28-9). This arrangement would be useful in any room where self-containment is an advantage – a guest room for example, or a bedroom for a teenager or an elderly relative.

wise. Sew the two strips together, then sew into a tube and add circular ends. Fill it with polystyrene granules. More traditional bolsters are usually filled with a firm pad.

To make the cover, cut a piece of fabric the width of the circumference of the pad by the pad's length, plus seam allowances. Your cover can have a plain, flat end, perhaps piped or with a frill set into the seam. For a gathered end, the simplest method is described below, but you can also gather by cutting a strip of fabric the length of the circumference of the pad by its radius, plus seam allowances. Join into a ring, then stitch one edge to the bolster tube. Sew gathering stiches along the other edge, pull up, and attach a covered button. This type of finish will benefit from piping sewn round the tube before attaching the ungathered end: you will get a much neater finish. Buttons covered in matching fabric can look very neat, but for a really dramatic effect use a silky tassle instead. Another variation might be to make your cylinder of fabric much longer than your pad so you can tie the ends close to the pad with ribbon or cord, Christmas cracker-like.

Gathered bolster ends

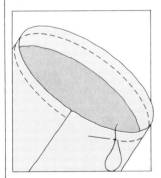

1. Right sides facing, stitch fabric into a cylinder. Fold in a 1.5cm (⅝in.) single hem at each end. Work gathering stitches by hand near edge.

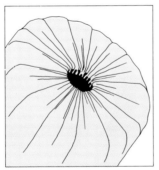

2. Insert cushion pad, centring it inside cover. At each end, pull up gathers tightly and evenly and fasten off gathering thread.

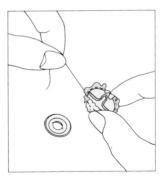

3. Cover two buttons by cutting circles of fabric and gathering round button shapes according to manufacturer's instructions.

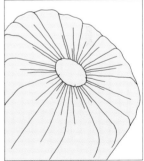

4. Using double thread, stitch buttons in place through their shanks over the central openings at each end of the bolster cover.

QUILTED COVERS

The technique of quilting, originally developed to anchor layers of fabric and padding together to provide thickness and warmth, can also be used to give an interesting surface texture to cushions. Since a light-weight fabric will be easiest to work with, you might like to use dressmaking fabric, which gives you a much wider range of plain and printed designs to choose from. Either quilt both the front and back of the cushion cover, or leave one side plain.

To make one quilted piece, first cut out a piece of your covering fabric slightly larger than required, then cut out a piece of backing fabric to the same size. Use an oddment of similar weight for this purpose, or buy a small amount of cotton lining. Finally, cut a piece of medium-weight synthetic wadding, again to the same size.

Decide how far apart you want the lines of quilting to fall, keeping in mind the size of the pattern repeat, and measure in this distance from the edge to arrive at the first quilting line. Stitch along this line, then continue across the fabric using the quilting bar on your machine to get the rows of stitching consistently spaced.

Once the quilting is finished, treat the fabric exactly as you would a single covering piece. You could make it up with a frill, with piping or with both; make a quilted bolster; or quilt a piece of fabric larger than your pad and make a cushion with a border as on pages 28-9 and 34-5. Don't always quilt on the straight of grain: quilt diagonally across the cushion, quilt a spiral from the centre out, on a geometric pattern quilt with it or against it, or quilt squares one inside the other (start from a small square in the centre and use a quilting bar to stitch squares moving progressively outwards). You can also use quilting techniques on novelty cushions (pages 38-9). A pile of cushions made from the same fabric would look particularly striking if they were all quilted in different patterns.

When you have mastered the simple grid technique, you might like to attempt more complex patterns, or try quilting around the motif on a patterned fabric.

Simple quilting

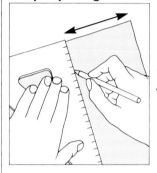

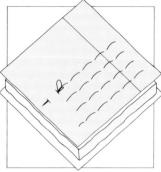

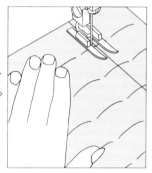

1. With a set square and a piece of tailors' chalk or a soft pencil, mark the first quilting line on the right side of one piece of fabric.

2. Place fabric to backing fabric with wrong sides facing, sandwiching a layer of wadding in between. Tack together in rows, matching raw edges.

3. Stitch through all three layers along the first quilting line already marked. Add the quilting bar to the sewing-machine.

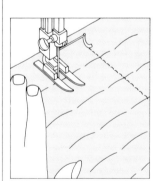

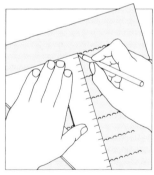

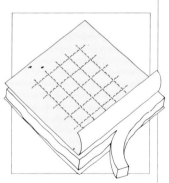

4. Set quilting bar guide to required spacing and position bar on first row of stitching. Stitch remaining rows across the fabric in the same way.

5. With set square against first row of stitching, mark first quilting line at right angles to the first set. Stitch this and remaining lines as before.

6. Trim wadding between fabric layers to 1.5cm (⅝in.) from outside stitching lines. Complete cushion cover in the usual way.

CUSHIONS WITH A DIFFERENCE

If you want your cushions to have a stronger impact than those made in simple shapes with ordinary fabric, search shops and markets for unusual coverings or use your imagination to create a collection of whimsical shapes.

Don't limit yourself to new fabrics for your covers – discarded curtains, tablecloths or articles of clothing can all be re-used. Old fabrics often have a softness and a lovely faded quality that you won't find in newer materials, and any stained or worn sections can be avoided (**1**). Market stalls specializing in old floor or table carpets will occasionally sell off damaged ones very cheaply, so consider transforming a plain sofa with a pile of exotic cushions made from sound portions of these.

If you can find a pretty, fold-over night-dress case, you'll have a ready-made cushion cover: just insert a pad of the right size and slipstitch round the edge (**2** and **3**). Look for lacy or embroidered tray cloths, antimacassars or table mats, and stitch them on to a plain backing. Sew two large handkerchiefs or printed scarves together (**4**); two square shawls would make a beautiful cover for a floor cushion.

Look at the objects around you to get ideas for novelty cushions. Children will love them and they make ideal presents, particularly when the cushion can be linked to a special interest or hobby.

For a complex shape like a shell (**5**), make a tracing paper template by copying an original. Quilt wadding on to the cover pieces before you sew them together.

The spherical shape needed for cherries (**6**), footballs etc., can be achieved by cutting the fabric in segments like an orange, or by taking large darts into the long sides of a rectangle of fabric. Cover rolled-up wadding for the 'twigs'.

A basic bolster construction forms the body of the pencil (**7**). To enable you to achieve the zigzagged join between body and shaped point, assemble all the sections flat and appliqué the decorative details before you stitch the cylinder closed. Stuff, then add the flat end with appliquéd 'lead'.

Make a child's seat in the shape of a house (**8**). A cube of foam forms the house, and a shaped piece the roof. Make covers for each section separately, and decorate with fabric paints before stitching together. Glue roof to house.

2 & 3

1

7

6

4

8

5

OCCASIONAL CHAIRS

Never meant to offer the same cradling softness as fully upholstered furniture, occasional chairs earn their keep by dint of their practicality: they are saving of money and space since they tend to be smaller, lighter and simpler in construction than their highly padded relations, and therefore not only cheaper but also easier to accommodate and to move – from room to room or simply in and out from under a dining table.

Those designs meant for long periods of use usually offer some degree of comfort despite a basically hard frame – by means of a seat and/or back made from a non-rigid material like leather or woven cane, a springy cantilevered construction or simply by the addition of a cushion or two. Dining chairs often have an unrelievedly hard surface, but since their periods of use are generally limited, this is not likely to cause major discomfort.

Because upholstered seating is such a major item of expenditure, it is easy to relegate these other types of chairs to second place, failing to give them the attention they deserve; yet they play a vital part in an overall seating scheme. If you are setting up your first home and space is at a premium, carefully chosen occasional chairs can provide plenty of inviting places for you and your guests to sit without contributing to the cluttered, suffocating atmosphere that too many heavily upholstered pieces often give to a small room. Later, when your home and your budget are larger, the versatility of these lighter designs is still invaluable; if you take care to choose comfortable dining chairs, for example, they can do extra duty in the bedroom, or living room. Remember also that your seating needs are likely to change so that a chair bought now to throw clothes over in the bedroom may one day be required for a more demanding purpose, so don't be tempted to settle for an attractive but very poor quality or impractical article.

The many types of occasional and dining chairs are discussed on the following pages.

Occasional chairs can fill many functions, from the extremely practical to the purely sybaritic, and this room contains a wide assortment: the bright red typist's chair with adjustable seat and back that gives maximum support through hours of paperwork; the dining chairs with arms and seat cushions that fit nicely around the table, yet do double duty in the sitting room; and the padded chaise that is best approached with a romantic novel and a bottle of wine.

CANE Today, as in our parents' and grandparents' time, some of the most attractive, adaptable and comfortable chairs are made from cane. Inexpensive and very light to move, cane chairs look right in any room – and are often found in the garden or on the patio as well. The addition of a squab seat or a few throw cushions will make the simple cane chair almost as comfortable as a much more expensive model. Similar in appearance to cane chairs, and often mistaken for them, Lloyd loom chairs are actually made by an ingenious process involving paper fibre, glue size and steel wire. These homely articles were widely manufactured right up to the 1960s, and it's still almost impossible to find a junk or secondhand shop without an example of Lloyd loom somewhere on the premises. Difficult to paint because of their woven constructions, both these types of chairs can be given a fresh new look with a can of car spray paint, which is available in a wide range of colours.

When buying secondhand, examine all pieces carefully to make sure there are no split sections or loose ends that may scratch the skin or snag the clothes of anyone who sits on them. Reject, too, very grimy woven chairs since you'll find it difficult to dislodge dirt from such tiny crevices.

LEATHER Although it has long been employed as a covering fabric, leather came to be widely used by itself as a chair seat or back during the 1920s when tubular steel was first developed for chair frame construction: many of the modern classic chairs designed in the Bauhaus school were made with this combinaton of materials. Although seating of this type is likely to be expensive, it has a beautifully restrained elegance and yet is strong enough to withstand extremely hard wear.

Ensure that the leather of any prospective purchase is still strong and supple, and examine it for small tears that could result in damage too great to repair. Sections of seam that have come unstitched, however, can be sewn up using a strong needle and thread. Check every section of a chrome frame for rust either on the surface or in and around the bolts that should be holding it together firmly.

WOOD The most traditional furnishing material of all, wood is difficult to surpass for toughness and good looks. Many family favourites – Windsor chairs, old-fashioned rockers and plain dining chairs, for example – are of solid wood construction. Even their most devoted admirers, however, would acknowledge that for use over long periods, chairs made of wood are greatly improved by the addition of cushions or a shaped seat pad (pages 48-9).

Check junk or antique shop finds to see that their joints are strong and there are no very deep dents or scratches. Then tap firmly on the surface of the wood – if a light-coloured dust appears, the item has woodworm and will need prompt treatment with a proprietary solution. Remember that the occupants of worm-ridden pieces allowed space in your home can easily colonize the floor and the woodwork as well

Far left: An early chrome and leather chair, Marcel Breuer's Wassily design (foreground) was inspired by bicycle handlebars. The chaise is a modernist version of a 19th-century shape.

Left: Traditional cane is equally at home indoors, outside or, as here, half-way between.

Below: An unusual combination – bentwood frame and leather-covered seat pad.

as other, possibly valuable or cherished, furnishing articles.

BENTWOOD Another furnishing classic, the bentwood chair was invented by a Czech, Michel Thonet, during the 1830s. Using steam to bend thin strips of bonded wood, he produced beautiful furniture at a low enough price to be available to ordinary people, then and now, and in large enough quantities to satisfy an enduring demand. Often made with woven cane seats, the bentwood rocker, the dining chair and the side chair with its distinctive sweeping arms look equally at home in modern or traditional rooms, and constitute wise seating buys in any terms.

Examine every section of an old bentwood design to make sure there are no splits, and look closely at the seat, especially if it is made of woven cane since torn or broken sections cannot be repaired and the seat will have to be recaned. Check for woodworm as described above.

DECK CHAIRS A firm favourite for outdoor use, the simple deck chair is extremely useful inside as well, for it can be brought out when numbers swell, and afterwards folded away out of sight. If you can't find a fabric design you like in the shops, it's a simple job to cover one yourself (page 55), using purpose-made canvas or any other material that will withstand considerable strain. If you have a pretty, old carpet with worn patches that make it unusable, cut it up and tack it to a deck chair frame to make a charming and unusual item of occasional seating.

DINING CHAIRS

Sharing a meal together is an important ritual of family life, and it is certainly one of the pleasantest ways to spend time with friends; but even delicious food and good conversation won't keep people around your table unless they are comfortable there.

Design

One of the most vital aspects of any dining chair is its relationship to the table with which it's to be used. If you are buying chairs on their own, note down all the dimensions of your table so you can take them into consideration. First of all, don't try to accommodate too many people, since cramped conditions will make it impossible for anyone to feel relaxed. Allow 700 mm (2¼ feet) for each diner, and the same amount of space for access between the back of the chair and a wall or another piece of furniture. Check that the distance between the chair seat and the underside of the table is large enough – 300 mm (12 in.) is about right – but if you like to sit with your legs crossed you will need more room still. If you are planning to put cushions of any kind on the seats, be sure to allow for this extra height. If at all possible, sit on the chair at its own table, or one of a similar height; when you rest your forearms on the surface, they should be parallel to the floor for maximum comfort. Many people prefer dining chairs with arms, but you'll have to allow a slightly wider space for this type. If you are short on room, check too that they will slide under the table when they're not in use.

Make sure the angle of the seat and back is comfortable for you and that the back is a good height – tall enough to give support without digging into your shoulder blades. The seat should be wide and deep enough to give plenty of support to the behind and thighs, and about 420 mm (16 in.) from the ground, but this will vary if members of your family tend to be taller or shorter than average.

Style

To a very large extent, the appearance of the dining chairs you choose will be governed by the function – or functions – of the room in which they will be used. Few of us have the luxury of a separate dining room these days – it's much more likely that meals are taken in the kitchen, in a part of the living room or even in a bedsitting room that must accommodate all domestic activities.

A formal dining room will demand a matching set of chairs, which don't need to have a particularly robust construction or durable fabric on the seats since they will probably not be subject to constant heavy wear. On the other hand, the chairs around a kitchen table that is the nerve-centre of the home and also doubles as an office, a sewing-room and a workshop will need to be particularly tough and adaptable, but in this setting there is no need for them to be a matching set. A cheerful jumble of junk shop finds and family treasures can look charming, as long as there is some unifying design

Right: A simple, informal dining area like this one looks fine fitted out with chairs of several different designs. Make your choice on the basis of availability or according to individual seating needs.

Below: A row of space-saving stools is just the job for hurried family breakfasts or quick snacks. They tuck neatly under the counter and are useful too when you need help to reach a high shelf.

element such as colour or period. An assortment of chairs like this would also cater for a variety of seating needs.

An informal kitchen is also an ideal place to consider bench seating, either built-in or free-standing (old church pews are perfect for this purpose). If space is tight, a built-in version could even conceal a roomy storage area under the seat. The great advantage of this solution is flexibility – many more bodies can be fitted in when you are entertaining, and children seem to be able to squeeze together in almost infinite numbers and enjoy the exercise hugely. On the minus side, the arrangement can be inconvenient, since no-one sitting in the middle can leave the table without disturbing everyone else. Avoid the type of benches that are fixed to the table as these can be particularly cumbersome.

In a room with a high-tech feel, or one where a lot of paperwork is dealt with, you might find that typists' chairs would work most efficiently. More expensive than dining chairs, those designed for office use can often be picked up secondhand. They offer good back support and their seat height is adjustable, so you can use them at a desk, a counter or an ironing board. Most office chairs are on castors as well, so they can be moved easily.

The dining table in many homes is in the living room, either placed in its own permanently-designated area (often the short arm of an L-shape), or pressed into its dining function only when required. In either case, unless your resources of space and furnishing are considerable, it would be wise to choose dining chairs that can also be used as occasional seating when you are entertaining larger numbers of people than usual. Look for those with arms and/or padded seats.

If you're desperately short of room, you may have to invest in folding chairs than can live under the bed or in a cupboard, and are brought out only when required. The traditional director's chair is ideal for this purpose, and be-cause it has arms and a fabric seat and back, it is more than averagely comfortable for both dining and occasional use. The greatest space-saver of all is the classic metal or wooden folding chair with an A-shaped frame, that packs away almost flat and can even be hung on the wall between meals.

Left: Classic bentwood dining chairs complement this sleek, modern table perfectly, yet they would sit just as happily under a more traditional version with turned legs and a scrubbed top.

Below: Store folding chairs away when they aren't being used.

Bottom: Comfortable cane chairs make this kitchen an inviting family meeting place.

SHAPED SEAT PADS

The easiest way to make your dining chairs more comfortable is to add simple, tie-on pads, shaped to fit their seats. These cushions can serve as a pretty furnishing accessory if you choose a covering fabric that co-ordinates with the curtains or blinds, or one that picks up one of the main colours in the room. Unlike throw cushions, seat pads like these usually get plenty of wear, so make sure your fabric is strong and closely-woven, or be prepared to renew the covers frequently.

When making shaped pads and covers, a paper template will ensure an accurate fit. Tracing paper is best as you can see through it, but newspaper or brown wrapping paper can be used too.

Your cushion will be anchored to the back struts with ties, and the number you need depends on the chair. The one in our picture needs four, but where your cushion is not shaped around the back strut you may be able to use just one, rather longer: fold it in half, then place the fold parallel with the raw edge of the cover piece and sew into the seam. Be bold and adventurous with the ties: for example, long, wide ones could be tied in enormous floppy bows; you could use ribbons instead of fabric; or make the ties and the piping in a different coloured fabric to the rest of the cover. It might be fun to make all the cushions for a set of chairs in the same fabric but with a different type – or colour – of tie on each one.

Add your fastening in the seam in the usual way, before you stitch the two cover pieces together. Slipstitching the opening closed is of course easier, but for these cushions it's worth taking the extra trouble to fit a fastening since you will want to remove the covers frequently for washing, especially if there are young children in the household.

Below are instructions for making the simplest of pads, but you could also make a shallow welted version following the instructions on pages 30-1. Pipe both cover pieces before you add the welt, and if possible set the ties into the welt seams at the back of the cushion: they will then be set in vertically. Set a zip into the seam joining welt to bottom cover piece, and position it at the back of the cushion.

A shaped seat pad

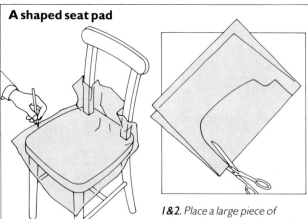

1&2. Place a large piece of tracing paper on seat and mark round the edges. Cut out template, replacing to mark position of back struts.

3. Using template, but adding 1.5cm (⅝in.) seam allowance all round, cut out two cover pieces. Reinforce back corners with a row of stitching.

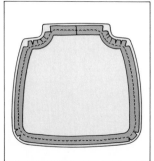

4. Make up enough piping in matching or contrasting fabric to go round cover. Attach to one cover piece in the usual way, notching at corners.

The addition of simple, shaped, tie-on cushions to your dining chairs will soften their appearance and encourage family and friends to linger and chat long after the last scraps of food have disappeared.

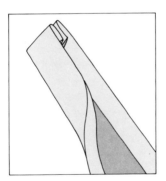

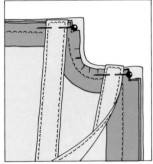

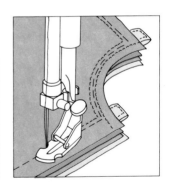

5. For each tie, cut a piece of fabric 30cm × 5cm (12in. × 2in.) and turn in 1cm (⅜in.) all round. Fold strip in half lengthwise and stitch all round.

6. Pin two completed ties over piping on right side of each back corner over previous stitching line, as shown in diagram.

7&8. Right sides facing, stitch two halves of cover together, catching in ties. Turn to right side. Insert pad, complete cover and tie on to seat.

DEEP SEAT CUSHIONS

Cushions to sit on or against, such as the seat and back cushions on a sofa, need to be substantially firmer than throw cushions, and are usually stuffed with very luxurious feather pads or, more cheaply, with suitably dense foam. The former will very probably have to be custom-made, while foam is quite awkward to cut at home, and you will be well advised to ask your dealer to shape it for you from a template. Either pad will be dense and substantial and will require a long zip in the cushion cover to accommodate it: this is inserted into the centre of the back welt and, on a square cushion, extends round each back corner for about 8cm (3in.). Seat cushions will sustain heavy wear, so strengthen the seams by adding piping to the covers.

Follow the instructions below for seat cushions on cane chairs, for deep cushions on a sofa with loose covers, and for substantial cushions to pad a windowseat or bench. You can, of course, stitch the zip into the seam between the welt and bottom cover piece, positioning it centrally at the back of the cushion: pipe the bottom cover piece first.

Deep seat cushions

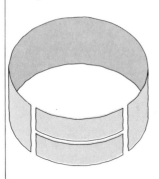

1. For round cover, cut welt in three sections as shown, with the strips on either side of the zip at least 8cm (3in.) longer than the zip.

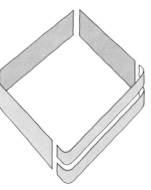

2. For square cover, cut five sections extending back welt strips for 8cm (3in.) along the adjoining sides to allow large opening.

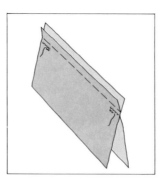

3. Right sides facing, tack two zip sections together. Stitch in for 4cm (1½in.) from each end, and fasten off, leaving central tacked section.

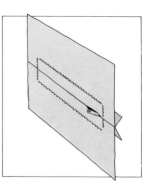

4. Centre zip behind tacked section, then pin and tack in place. Stitch from right side of fabric in usual way. Leave zip closed.

The technique of adding a gusset or welt to your cushion cover to accommodate its depth works equally well for both modern and traditional styles.

Far left: The neat, welted construction of these custom-made seat and back cushions helps them achieve their cool geometric shapes as well as their upholstery-like softness.

Left: Thinner pads add colour and comfort to a set of cane dining chairs. These cushions are piped and shaped to fit the chair seats, but the method of construction is exactly the same.

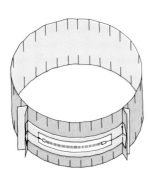

5. *For a round cover, pin and stitch welt pieces into a ring. Snip notches into seam allowance on both edges spaced 2.5cm (1 in.) apart.*

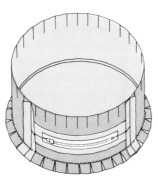

6. *Open zip. Right sides facing, pin welt to cover piece, which you have already piped. Stitch, then stitch welt to other, piped, cover piece.*

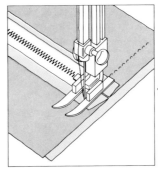

7. *For a square cover, stitch welt sections together, right sides facing, leaving 1.5cm (⅝in.) open at each end of front seams.*

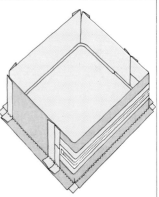

8. *Snip into seam allowances at back corners of welt. Open zip and pin welt to piped cover piece. Stitch welt to each cover piece in turn.*

A BUTTONED LINING

Used in conjunction with a deep, shaped seat cushion (pages 50-1), a padded lining for a cane or Lloyd loom chair will offer a degree of comfort approaching that of an upholstered armchair – prettily, and with very little effort on your part.

To begin with, make a paper template. If the back and arms of your chair are more or less at right angles to the seat you can cut your cover pieces in a single section, as in the photograph; but if the back tapers in, cut the template and your fabric into three pieces as shown below.

Use synthetic wadding or foam as padding, cut in one piece. This padding is anchored in place with covered buttons, attached through the lining with strong thread or twine, and using a large darning needle or a double bayonet needle (a needle that has a point at both ends).

Stitch your cover to the chair, or make ties and sew them into the seams at the top corners and arms (pages 48-9).

Following the instructions, right, try buttoning throw cushions: those with frills or welts (pages 22-3 and 30-1), might look particularly smart with buttons through the middle.

Buttoning

1. Thread one button shank on to about 1m (40in.) of twine, then thread both ends of twine through a large needle and push through cover from front to back.
2. Turn pad over, remove one end of twine from needle and thread on another button.
3. Remove needle and make a slip knot (see below).
4. Pull tightly, secure with a reef knot, then trim twine under button.

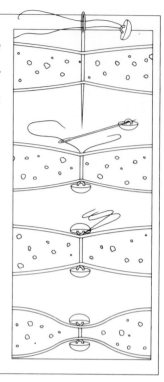

A buttoned, fitted chair lining

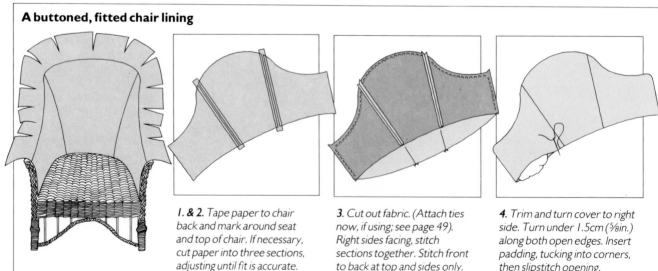

1. & 2. Tape paper to chair back and mark around seat and top of chair. If necessary, cut paper into three sections, adjusting until fit is accurate.

3. Cut out fabric. (Attach ties now, if using; see page 49). Right sides facing, stitch sections together. Stitch front to back at top and sides only.

4. Trim and turn cover to right side. Turn under 1.5cm (⅝in.) along both open edges. Insert padding, tucking into corners, then slipstitch opening.

Right: Plain, closely-woven cotton provides the ideal surface on which to stencil a pretty motif that can be used on its own or chosen to echo other patterns in the room. Here, an enthusiastic practitioner of the technique has been let loose on the walls, the curtains, the lampshade, the dresser and the bedcover, as well as the padded cane chair.

5. Mark desired position of buttons, then attach pairs of self-covered shank buttons (page 35 and above). Stitch cover to chair, or tie it on.

DECK AND DIRECTOR'S CHAIRS

For value, good looks and practicality, few items of seating score higher than those classic folding chairs in canvas and wood, the deck chair and the director's chair. Many well-loved examples have sound frames even if their covers are torn, dirty or faded. Remove the old cover by easing out the original tacks with a mallet and small chisel. Then measure the frame and cut out your fabric, hemming it down the sides if you are not using deck chair canvas, which comes in a specially narrow width. For a director's chair you will also need an eyelet kit: cut holes in the correct position in the fabric, insert the eyelet and bang down hard with a hammer or other tool. The screw and butterfly nut will fit through these holes.

If you have always been put off using deck or director's chairs indoors by the limited designs of deck chair canvas, look for interesting alternatives. You might quilt a fabric you like on to canvas, with wadding in between: follow the instructions on pages 36-7. Or look for an old oriental carpet that is worn or damaged in places: you might be able to salvage a piece large enough to make an unusual cover.

Above: Stripes are the order of the day in this sunny, nautical bathroom. The boldest of all are reserved for a smart director's chair that provides comfortable seating in a tight corner, and is a catch-all for clothes.

Cover for a director's chair

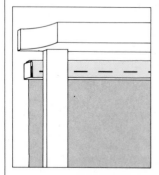 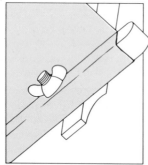

1. Position seat canvas on frame so raw edges are at sides. Turn these under and staple canvas around side rails at 3cm (1 ¼in.) intervals.

2. For back, wind canvas around struts and staple in place as before. Hold strut and canvas to frame with screw and wing nut.

Below: Some of the nicest deck chairs are covered with crisp white canvas to set off the golden glow of the wood, a combination echoed throughout this country dining room.

Above: Almost everything in this ad hoc dining room can be folded away to clear a path for traffic. The ever-practical deck chair waits patiently until it is needed, taking up virtually no room at all.

Cover for a deck chair

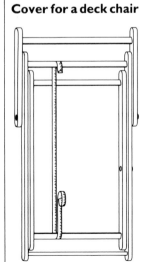

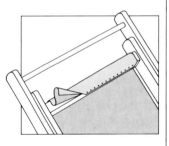

To estimate canvas, lie the frame flat. Measure between end rails, allowing 2cm (¾in.) at each end for fixing. Turn under raw edges and anchor canvas with tacks 5cm (2in.) apart, beginning in the middle and working outwards.

UPHOLSTERED FURNITURE

Added cushions may do much to soften the rigid look and feel of an unpadded chair, but there is little to rival the comfort of properly upholstered furniture, whether this is a set of elegantly-covered dining chairs or a fully sprung sofa. The deep and relaxing comfort we expect from our sofas and armchairs was, however, an unknown luxury not so very long ago. In medieval times, seating consisted of stone slabs that were part of the fabric of the building, and for centuries after that only thin layers of tapestry or fabric came between a hard seat and its occupant. It was not until the eighteenth century that formal upholstery techniques were put into practice – and many of these were not originally intended to be used for domestic seating. When more and more padding, usually horsehair, came to be added to the seat, back and arms of wooden chairs (these areas blending together to form the shapes with which we are familiar), new methods had to be found to keep the additional material in place, and many of these were adapted from saddle-making skills already in use. Later, the technique of buttoning, which had first been developed to provide comfort in the coaches that travelled the appalling roads of the time, was applied to ordinary chairs in an effort to improve them. Whatever their origins, the traditional upholstery skills that were developed nearly 250 years ago – with the single exception of the coil spring, invented in 1828 – are those we use today, and the styles of most of our modern sofas and chairs are a product of this craftsmanship.

Design
The manufacturing and selling of furniture would be greatly simplified if one shape or style were universally agreed to be 'comfortable'. Unfortunately, we differ as widely in our seating requirements as we do in every other area of our lives. If you have small children, for example, beautifully upholstered dining chairs with padded seats, backs and arms are likely to

The fiercest of winters could be endured happily from the enveloping warmth and cosiness of a room like this. The seating, like all its elements, has been chosen with a sure eye for line and colour, and constructed using superb materials and traditional techniques to ensure an unsurpassable standard of comfort and durability.

Left: People's needs often differ widely, even within the same family, so never feel that all your chairs and sofas should be chosen from the same range. The items of seating in this informal room all differ in the height of their seats and backs, in their depth and in the style of their arms.

Right: Adaptable unit seating is an efficient way to deal with small rooms that have to accommodate seating for large numbers of people. Many ranges include a special unit that folds out to make a single bed.

acquire unwelcome accretions such as gobbets of porridge and scuff marks from tiny feet, so you will save yourself a lot of heartbreak if you pick something that can be easily washed or wiped clean.

When it comes to more heavily upholstered items, make sure the designs you choose reflect the way you and your family sit, plus the heights and ages of all the members of the household. For example, people who like to curl up in the corner of a sofa and rest their arms along the back will appreciate a wide, deep seat and a low back; those who prefer to sit fairly upright need to have their head and neck supported, so a seating range with a firm, high back would be the best choice. If you like to stretch out fully to read or to watch television, look for plenty of length and low, wide arms

that will serve as head-rests. Tall people need deep, high seats so that their knees do not come up to meet their chins when they sit down; short people have the opposite problem – if the chair is too deep they cannot sit back properly, and if it is too high, their legs will dangle above the floor.

Older people (and many younger ones) find very low seating difficult to get out of, so if you have to cater for elderly friends and relatives, keep this in mind. It's easy to see that each member of the household could have completely different seating requirements, and if this is the case, consider buying several small sofas and chairs of different designs, rather than a huge three- or four-seater. In fact, you may find a large-scale sofa out of proportion in a smallish room, or clumsy and inflexible in terms of the furniture's positioning:

smaller pieces can more easily be re-arranged to cope with changing social requirements and often make it possible for space to be used more efficiently.

If flexibility is your main requirement, consider buying unit seating – modular side or corner pieces that can be moved around and joined together in any number of ways: two corner units together make a small sofa, two corner units separated by a side unit make a three-seater and so on. This system has many advantages, not the least of which is that it allows you to start furnishing modestly, with two or three pieces, then add to these gradually as space and budget allow, keeping in mind that a very long gap between purchases would result in uneven wear. Some of these units have matching armchairs and pouffes.

Construction

Some seating ranges, especially those at the top end of the market, are still made in the traditional way, with vertically-positioned, individual coil springs supported on webbing and covered with complex layers of padding. Much modern upholstery, however, is constructed using easier, cheaper methods that involve the use of foam, though often seat or back cushions have only a core of this material, which is wrapped in a layer of synthetic fibre to make it soft and resilient. Seat cushions should, of course, be firmer than back ones, so they often contain a denser quality of foam or a different proportion of foam to fibre. Very inexpensive seating is usually filled with solid or crumbled foam only. The most common supporting structure is either rubber webbing or horizontally-linked tension springing, stretched across the seat and back frame; but some of the cheapest modern ranges consist simply of blocks of foam, or perhaps two blocks glued together, sculpted to the right shape and covered with a loose cover. They have a chunky shape.

Size and position

Because much upholstered seating is covered in the customer's choice of fabric (and is therefore unreturnable), it's particularly important that you make absolutely certain not only that your chosen sofa or chair will fit into your room so that there is at least 600 mm (2 feet) of leg room in front and the same amount of space at the back for traffic, but also that there will be no problems with access. No matter how large your room is, an enormous sofa may have to be ruled out if it won't go through the front door or up the stairs to your flat.

When you are arranging your seating, try not to line the wall with it or you risk creating the atmosphere of a public waiting room. People converse most easily sitting at right angles to, or facing, each other, so some kind of L- or U-shaped arrangement is ideal. Again, this will be easier to achieve with several smaller items than one or two larger ones. If television viewing is an important activity in your household, make sure everyone in the main seating area can see the set clearly.

Covers

Upholstered furniture has two types of covering: fitted covers or loose covers. Fitted covers give a formal impression since they have a tight, tailored look that comes from being stretched into place and tacked to the wooden frame; the tacks are then hidden by braid or piping. In general, these covers cost less than loose ones, but the fact that they are under constant tension means they often wear out more quickly and you will sometimes find that a fabric labelled suitable for loose covers hasn't enough strength to recommend it for fitted ones – check the label or ask for advice.

Loose covers give a much more relaxed effect and some even have a ruffled or pleated valance around the bottom.

Above: Choose pale, plain upholstery fabric to set off dramatic colours or patterns elsewhere in the room. Remember that loose covers are easiest to keep clean.

Left: If your sofa has a patterned cover (a wise choice where there are children in the household or, as here, when its location makes it vulnerable to dirt), keep the room's other elements as understated as possible.

They are cut out in pieces, then sewn together like a dress, with an opening that may be fastened with hooks and bars, velcro or a zip to allow the cover to slip over the sofa or chair; cushion covers are made in the same way. This type of cover can be removed for cleaning and even changed to suit the seasons or your mood, if the budget will stretch to two or more sets of covers for the same item. Some furniture, however, is not suitable for this treatment: straight, simple shapes are best, so if your sofa or chair has lots of curves and embellishments, you will have to give it a tight cover.

Colour and pattern

Large items of seating are bound to dominate any room they occupy, so think carefully about the fabric you choose to cover them. Avoid currently fashionable colours, very bright shades or intrusive patterns of any kind. However attractive these may appear at the outset, you will soon tire of them and have to decide whether to live with something you dislike, or waste money buying new covers before they're needed.

Curb, too, any desire for a whimsical motif or one that is jokey or childish; daily exposure to these visual witticisms can become intensely irritating. You can afford to be more adventurous with pieces of furniture that are on display for a limited period only, such as dining chairs in a separate room.

Make sure the scale of any print you choose is right for your furniture and your room – a small pattern will look fine on a large sofa or in a large room, but an enormous one on a modestly-sized chair or in a tiny room could be disastrous. Children and pets call for a design that will not show dirt, so pick a dark colour or a random print since small and regular ones (tiny checks or pinstripes, for example) will show spots as clearly as plain, light colours.

Safety

It is important that your seating (especially if it contains foam) and the fabric you choose to cover it has been treated for fire resistance. This is particularly vital if it will be used by young children, elderly people or smokers.

FABRICS AND FIBRES

In addition to enhancing the look of your rooms, the textiles you choose to cover your seating must withstand constant wear, so be as particular when it comes to selecting a suitable fibre as you are about pattern and colour; a mistake could mean wasting not only money, but all the time and care you have spent in covering your sofa or seat cushion. By law, every fabric must be marked with its fibre content, so check the labels before you make a decision, and once you have made your choice, note down the correct cleaning methods.

Textile fibres are either natural or man-made; the natural ones come from plants (like linen or cotton) or from animals (like silk and wool). Some man-made fibres have their origins in nature too, but not in a form that is usable for this purpose. Viscose, which is made from the cellulose material in wood, is the best-known of these. While such naturally-based fibres are known as regenerated, those produced from inert raw materials like coal and oil are called synthetic.

Natural fibres

Because they come from living sources, many natural fibres are becoming scarcer and more expensive.

WOOL has many advantages as a furnishing fabric: it has strength and resilience that help it maintain its appearance for long periods; a highly absorbent quality so it takes dye readily; a built-in flame resistance and a softness and warmth that make it extremely comfortable to sit on. Another practical consideration is its tendency to repel dirt.

Make sure all woollen fabric is treated with a moth-proofing solution. Dry clean it when it gets grubby and sponge small spots without over-wetting.

The suitability of a woollen fabric for fixed covers is determined by the weight and the weave, so ask for advice.

COTTON can also be dyed (and printed) easily and it is often treated to make it shrink- and fade-resistant. Most often used for loose covers, this fibre must be made into a very thick, strong and closely woven material if it is to be used for fixed covers or for seat cushions.

LINEN (flax) on its own is not the most practical of furnishing fabrics. Coarser than cotton, it creases badly and loses strength when wet. It is sold most commonly in a mix with cotton (called linen union) which comes in an enormous range of prints and plain colours.

SILK is not strong enough to be used on chairs and sofas, but it is sometimes mixed with linen or cotton to make it more durable. Expensive to produce, silk has a distinctive sheen.

Artificial fibres

Fibres created by science are valuable to us both to substitute for the increasingly hard-to-obtain natural ones, and to supplement natural fibres and give them properties they would not have on their own.

VISCOSE (also called viscose rayon), as we have seen, is the most widely-used regenerated fibre. A strong material, it loses this strength quickly when wet (sponge carefully) and so is often combined with other fibres.

Of the synthetic fibres, NYLON was the first and remains the most well known. It is also widely used in combination with natural or other synthetic fibres, since it has an unfortunate clammy smell and feel on its own. It is very light, strong and stain-resistant (the modern 'fourth generation' nylons such as Antron are particularly good in this respect), but once marks are embedded they can be difficult to remove, so wash items made from this material frequently. Trade names are Bri-nylon, Celon, Enkalon, Perlon, Antron, Rilsan and Nomex.

POLYESTER, similarly strong and durable, is also light and crease-resistant and washes particularly well. Polyester fabrics are sold as Terylene, Trevira, Terlenka and Dacron.

ACRYLIC fabrics tend to resemble wool and are often blended with it for furnishing purposes. They are strong, stain-resistant and able to retain their shape well. Available under the trade names Courtelle, Acrilan, Orlon and Dralon (a fibre that is often woven to imitate velvet), acrylics will melt rather than burn at high temperatures.

MODACRYLICS (acrylics that have been modified for flame resistance) are similar in appearance and also tend to be blended with wool, but they shrink easily so take care to wash and iron them at low temperatures. Look for the trade names Dynel or Teklan.

Deep, glowing colours like those
used so brilliantly in the fabric
covering this graceful, curving
sofa are always easier to achieve
on fabrics woven from natural
fibres than on those made with
synthetic ones, which are not as
absorbent and therefore less
receptive to dye.

NEW COVERS FOR OLD

Many dining or occasional chairs are made using the traditional skills of upholstery to provide padding where it is needed most – on the seat particularly, but also on the arms and back. Stripping down and rebuilding this padding, especially on arms and sprung seats, is a reasonably complex task and one we haven't attempted to tackle here. Simply re-covering the arms and seat, however, involves few specialist skills and no specialist tools, and renewing the back completely is a job well within the scope of the amateur: with very little work and almost no outlay beyond the cost of the fabric, you will be able to transform dramatically a worn or secondhand set of chairs, or even those that have grown too familiar over the years.

When removing the old cover, work in the direction of the wood grain and take care not to split the wood, especially if the chair is old and delicate. Use the old cover as a guide when estimating fabric for the new one. Choose a fabric of suitable weight and weave, and cut it on the straight of grain in such a way that any pattern is centred on the chair's seat or back; for a seat, the cover will need to be large enough to hang down all round for about 5cm (2in.) below the rail of the chair.

Add a layer of wadding over the old calico, then attach the new cover using 13mm (½in.) fine tacks. Make sure your cover fits smoothly over the padding by driving each tack into the wood only a short distance first (temporary tacking). Begin at the centre of the back rail, move to the centre of the front rail, then tack the sides, also in the centre and also temporarily. Gradually work outwards from the centre of each rail, pulling the fabric tight as you go: eliminate wrinkles by removing tacks, adjusting the fabric, then re-tacking. Only when the corners are finished and the cover lies absolutely smooth over the seat should you go on to drive the tacks home, and carefully trim away any excess fabric close to the tacks. You can then attach braid or gimp over the tack heads using fabric adhesive – but don't feel constrained by tradition. On page 67 are some suggestions for varying the ways you finish off your chair, and you can carry these over to the back and arms as well.

If you are intending to do more than a little work of this

type, such as re-covering a whole set of dining chairs for example, you will almost certainly find it worth your while to hire a pair of low trestles for each chair to rest on while you work. Bending over or sitting on the floor for long periods will be very uncomfortable, and a table top is really too high for this purpose.

Similarly, a magnetic hammer will repay its initial cost in time saved if you are dealing with a number of chairs; the head picks up tacks so you can place them directly on the wood without handling them. Professional upholsterers fling a handful of tacks into their mouths, then spit each one on to the hammer as it's needed!

The techniques used in upholstery are suitable not only for fully-padded seating, but also for small areas on occasional chairs, where they provide some comfort, yet leave the wood as the main focus of interest. Larger hall or living room models often have padded arms and back as well as an upholstered seat (above), while dining chairs are usually padded on the seat only (right).

RE-COVERING AN UPHOLSTERED SEAT

Re-covering an upholstered seat

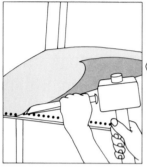

1. Working in the direction of the grain and using a mallet and a ripping chisel, carefully remove the tacks anchoring the old cover.

2. Place a layer of wadding on top of the seat, over the old inner cover. Cut into the wadding at the back corners to ease it around struts.

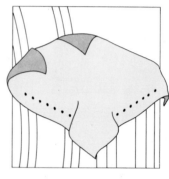

3. Cut out a piece of covering fabric slightly larger than needed and tack it into place temporarily along outside face of chair rails.

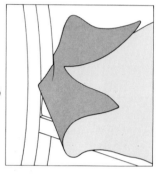

4. At back struts, fold back fabric over seat and make a diagonal cut into fabric from corner to within 6mm (¼in.) of strut.

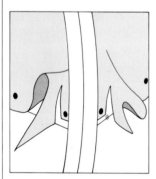

6. Tuck the fabric neatly around the strut and pull down tightly. Tack next to the strut and trim close to the tack. Trim equally from each side.

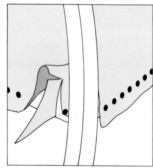

7. Tuck fabric under and fold down, parallel to back strut. Adjust until fabric is flat and fold is straight, then tack in place.

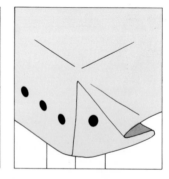

8. For square front corners, pull side fabric round to front rail and tack. Form pleat with front fabric in line with chair corner and tack over first tack.

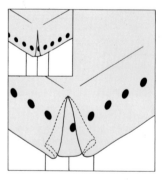

9. For rounded front corners, pull down fabric over corner and tack. Fold fabric on each side in, fold towards corner, and tack in place.

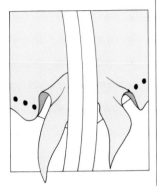

5. Ease the two resulting tongues of fabric down carefully on either side of each strut, between the strut and the main seat section.

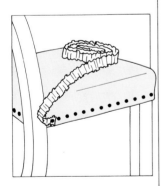

10. Adjust cover; hammer tacks home. Trim fabric close to tacks. Tack end of braid to back corner; fold braid back over tack. Glue round seat.

Four ways to conceal tacks: with a narrow strip of matching or contrasting fabric, a length of purpose-made braid or a piece of ribbon, tied prettily at the corners.

A PADDED CHAIR BACK AND ARMS

Padding a chair back

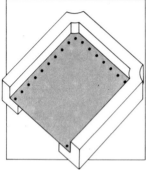

1. Working from the front, tack fabric, wrong side up, close to frame's inner edge, spacing tacks 2.5cm (1 in.) apart. (Cross section shown.)

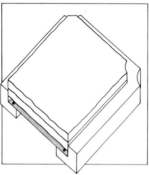

2. Cut two pieces of wadding to fit inside frame precisely and tuck into position over fabric. The fabric will hold wadding in place.

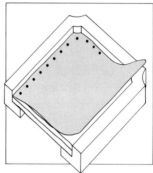

3. On top of wadding, tack second piece of fabric right side up, as close as possible to corner. Trim off excess fabric with a sharp knife.

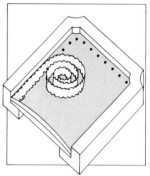

4. Using fabric adhesive, cover tacks with matching or contrasting braid or gimp, easing it around curves and mitring corners.

Re-covering padded arms

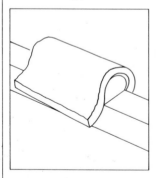

1. Cut a piece of wadding large enough to go round arm over existing padding. Anchor with tacks spaced at 2.5cm (1 in.) intervals.

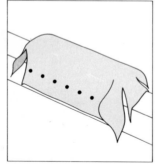

2. Cut a piece of covering fabric slightly larger than wadding. Anchor with tacks along sides. Cut into fabric at corners as shown.

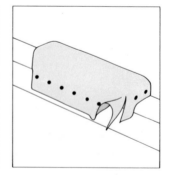

3. At ends, pull fabric down between frame and padding. Tack. At corners, tuck fabric up along sides of arm to make a neat vertical pleat, and tack.

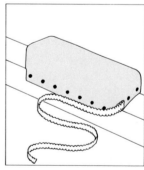

4. Trim away excess fabric, if necessary. Tack end of braid on at back, then turn back on itself and glue over tacks all round.

RENEWING A DROP-IN SEAT

Although rebuilding a drop-in seat is a more complex project than simply re-covering a sprung seat, it is still not difficult and can be very rewarding.

Lift the drop-in seat out of the chair by removing any small dowels or screws holding it in place, then tapping it from underneath. You will see that the basic support for the seat is webbing running in each direction. Replacing this with new webbing (black and white is the best quality) requires more leverage than can be obtained by hand, and a webbing stretcher will give you a great advantage. Keeping the webbing on the roll, push a loop of it through the hole in the stretcher from underneath, with the handle of the stretcher pointing towards the centre of the frame. Place the stretcher bar through the loop, then stretch the webbing over the rails by pulling the handle towards you. If a stretcher is unobtainable, wrap the webbing lengthwise over a block of wood about 20cm (8in.) long and roughly the width of the webbing, and lever it against the rail.

Other materials and tools you will need are two sizes of tack – 20mm (⅝in.) improved ones for the hessian and 10mm (⅜in.) ones for the cover; 10 or 12oz hessian, cut in two pieces slightly larger than the frame; a reel of upholsterer's twine and a half-circle needle to make the bridle ties (step **6**); mixed animal hair or upholstery fibre; calico and synthetic wadding; and your covering fabric.

Drop-in seats can also be renewed with foam. Replace webbing and hessian as in steps **1** to **5**, then cut some 5cm (2in.) thick foam to the same size as the frame. Bevel its bottom edge by cutting a 2.5cm (1in.) strip off all round the perimeter. Cut strips of cotton fabric 10cm (4in.) wide and slightly longer than the sides of the foam, fold them in half lengthwise and stick one half to the uncut top edge of the foam – the edge of the fabric should be 5cm (2in.) from that of the foam. Place the foam on the hessian, stuck sides uppermost, turn the frame over and tack the other edge of the strips of fabric to the underside of the frame temporarily. Pulling down hard will give you a nice even dome; when you are satisfied, hammer the tacks home, then cover with calico and fabric as in steps **13-16**.

This beautifully-crafted antique highchair uses the standard drop-in seat construction to provide a charming mealtime perch for the youngest member of the family. On a tiny seat like this you would need only four strips of webbing.

Renewing a drop-in seat

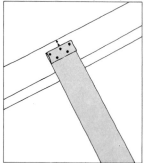

I. Fold up a 2.5cm (1in.) hem on webbing. Tack to centre of back rail 1.3cm (½in.) from edge with five tacks placed in a 'W' shape.

2. Thread a loop of webbing through the hole in the stretcher and pull towards you over centre of front rail, so it is taut but not unduly stressed.

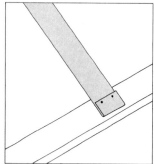

3. Anchor with a row of three tacks. Cut webbing, leaving 2.5cm (1in.) excess. Turn this back over existing tacks and add two more to make 'W'.

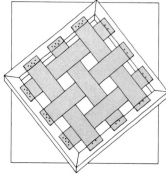

4. Add one strip of webbing on either side of first in the same way, then repeat across width of frame, interweaving strips as shown.

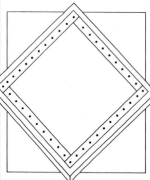

5. Cut a piece of hessian the same size as the seat. Turn up 1cm (⅜in.) on each edge and tack in position spacing tacks about 4cm (1½in.) apart.

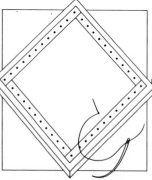

6. Cut a length of twine 1½ times seat perimeter. Make a 2.5cm (1in.) stitch in the centre of one side, 7.5cm (3in.) from edge. Knot to anchor.

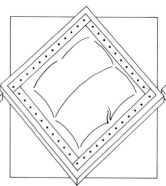

7. Take a stitch at nearest corner, then at centre of adjacent rail and so on, making two loops of about 20cm (8in.) along each side. Knot end.

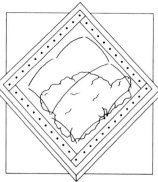

8. Tease out fibre and tuck evenly and tightly under and around bridle ties until you build up 5cm (2in.) thickness all over, with a domed centre.

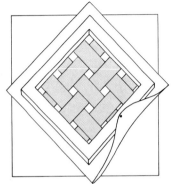

9. Cut a piece of calico 5cm (2in.) larger than seat. Place calico over seat, then turn over. Anchor to the centre of each rail with temporary tacks.

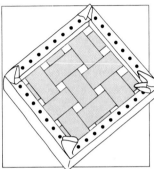

10. Smoothing calico as you go, add temporary tacks along each rail, spacing them about 5cm (2in.) apart. Make sure no fibre escapes over edge.

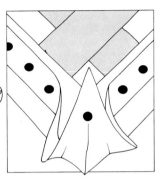

11. At each corner, pull calico taut over corner point and tack. Fold calico at each side of tack into a pleat, trimming away excess calico.

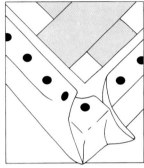

12. Fold in pleats at each side and anchor with a tack. Check that calico is smooth and taut. Drive tacks home. Trim calico close to tacks.

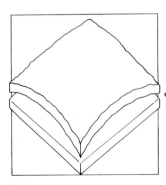

13. Turn seat over. Cut a piece of wadding to fit top of seat precisely and lay it down: it will be held in place by the top cover.

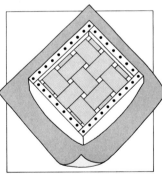

14. Measure seat both ways and cut out a piece of covering fabric 5cm (2in.) larger all round. Make sure pattern is centred. Turn seat over.

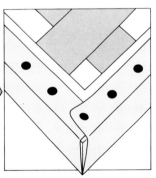

15. Anchor top fabric to centre of rail on each side with temporary tack. Smooth fabric over seat and temporary tack. Fold in corners as before.

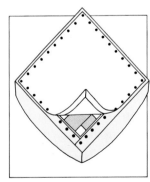

16. Drive tacks home. Cut a piece of hessian 1cm (⅜in.) larger all round than underside of frame. Turn under 1cm (⅜in.) all round and tack.

THROW-OVER COVERS

Whether you choose this casually-draped style because you like its soft, informal look, or to compensate for a lack of sewing skills, you'll find it suits many decorating tastes.

Begin with a chair or sofa that has a sound frame and padding – sturdy old pieces can often be culled from relations or bought cheaply at secondhand shops. Many new ranges come covered only in calico, and an item from one of these makes a good basis for a no-sew cover.

The easiest covering to buy is fabric by the metre – plain or quilted – which is available in a huge choice of colours and textures. The only stitching involved is a simple hem along each edge or perhaps a seam joining two widths.

Look too at flat double sheets, which come in an array of colours and patterns, or try a soft blanket for a warm, cosy effect. A pretty rug could camouflage a tatty armchair, while a huge tablecloth might suit a two- or three-seater sofa. Look out for beautiful bedspreads as well.

The soft, resilient layers of padding in a quilt make it an ideal throw-over cover.

Right: A huge bedspread tucks neatly around the chunky form of a modern sofa in this restrained interior. The simple square pattern of the quilting echoes the geometric shapes in the Kelim rug that features so largely in the room's design.

Below: On a smaller scale, this daintily sprigged cot coverlet has been draped simply, but to great effect, over a delightful wooden loveseat.

The first domestic textiles were tapestries and shawls tossed over stools or benches to make them softer and less chilling, and this is still a very appealing furnishing style, quite apart from the fact that no sewing skills whatsoever are needed to achieve it.

Layer richly-coloured and patterned fabrics to create an opulent, baroque setting (above and far right) or choose a single plain material if you prefer a more tranquil, 20th-century environment (right).

MAINTENANCE

If you want the seating in which you have invested so much thought and expense to remain in good condition as long as possible, make sure you know the right way to take care of it.

Cushions

Shake out feather cushions frequently and try to air them outside from time to time. If you are very careful, it is possible to wash feather pads in warm water, but this is an awkward task as they may take several days to dry and they need to be shaken often during this time. Washing also removes some of the natural resilience from feathers, so dry cleaning is better.

Wash foam cushions in their covers, squeezing gently in warm suds. Rinse each cushion several times; press out as much water as possible, then wrap it in a towel and press again. Foam cushions should be dried in a warm place, but keep them away from direct heat since hot foam can give off toxic fumes.

Cushions with a synthetic filling can be washed by machine and tumble dried. Do not dry clean them since their filling will absorb and hold toxic fumes from the cleaning fluid.

Occasional furniture

The appearance and serviceability of chairs with an exposed frame will be greatly improved if the material from which they're made is treated kindly.

CANE AND WICKER furniture will rot if it is exposed to damp, so never leave it out for extended periods or overnight – even if there is no rain, the morning dew will take its toll.

When the cane becomes grubby, brush out the surface dirt, using a toothbrush for really awkward corners, then scrub the chair with warm soapy water. Leave it to dry naturally – ideally in the sun – then finish with a little neutral furniture polish. Very pale cane can be kept that way with a weak solution of domestic bleach.

WOOD The variety of woods used for making chairs is enormous so try to find out which wood – or at least which type of wood – you are dealing with.

Waxed pieces (often beech or elm) will be glad of an additional coat of wax occasionally, sparingly applied, then buffed to a deep shine with a soft cloth.

Painted wood should be wiped with warm water and detergent, then dried and finished with a proprietary furniture cream. For ingrained dirt, try a cream bathroom cleanser or a little scouring powder.

Oiled finishes such as teak or iroko should have a little purpose-made oil rubbed into them occasionally. Make sure the surface is dust-free first and don't use too much oil or a sticky residue will be left to attract more dust.

All wood is harmed by constant exposure to fierce heat, so try to keep furniture away from radiators, hot-air ducts and fires. If possible, install a humidifier, or place bowls of water around in winter. Try not to spill any alcohol (perfume included) on a wood finish – if you do, wipe it up immediately.

PLASTIC Wash plastic chairs with warm water and detergent. Do not rub excessively or you will increase static, which attracts dust. Avoid abrasive cleaners, since they will cause scratches in which stains and dirt can become imbedded.

CHROME Wipe with warm soapy water and use a soft cloth for drying, or try paraffin, dry baking soda or an ammonia solution. Do not use an abrasive cleaner.

Upholstery

Direct sunlight, especially when it is magnified by glass, weakens all fabrics and will eventually cause colours to fade, so try to position sofas and chairs away from windows, or protect them with blinds or net curtains.

Don't let children jump on your upholstery – the springs will never survive such treatment. Keep small feet (and large ones) completely away since shoe buckles can catch in the fabric and hard soles will wear it through and grind in dirt. Animal claws can do serious damage as well. Discourage people from perching on the arms of your sofas and chairs, as they may damage the supporting structure.

Treat new items with a protective spray like Scotchguard to keep them clean as long as possible. Brush regularly or vacuum with the appropriate upholstery attachment to remove dust and crumbs. Don't leave this task for your annual spring-clean – the dirt will have become ingrained and almost

Most cane furniture is exceptionally lightweight and easy to carry, so there is no excuse for leaving it outside overnight so damp and dew can take their toll.

Leather, like many woods, should be wiped with a soft cloth wrung out in warm soapy water. Rinse with clear water, then dry. Finally, apply a proprietary cream or hide food to keep it soft and supple and prevent cracking; saddle soap will do the same job. Suede finishes require a special cleaner sold only for this material.

Plastic covers, such as those made from PVC, should never be cleaned with polish, since spirit of any kind removes the constituent that keeps the material supple, causing it to become dry and brittle very quickly. Here again, use warm soapy water (*never* an abrasive), then rinse, or try a car upholstery cleaner.

REPAIRS If you don't catch it in time, the smallest tear or hole in a chair cover could snag on a button or zip and turn into a major repair job, so deal with any small accidents immediately and look over your seating from time to time in case any such weaknesses have developed without being noticed.

Simple tears in a loose cover can be repaired from the back using iron-on patching tape. Those in fixed covers should be slip-stitched together using strong matching thread and an upholsterer's half-circle needle. To do this, anchor the edges of the torn fabric together with darning needles pushed firmly into the padding – if these edges are very frayed, you may need to turn under a tiny hem. Knot the thread and insert the needle into the underside of the fabric to conceal the knot. Fasten the two edges together with tiny stitches, pulling the thread firmly each time.

To patch a small hole, you will need a piece of the covering fabric slightly larger than the hole – make sure your patch matches any pattern or pile on the cover. If you don't have any extra fabric, you might be able to cut a small piece from a section of the chair that is normally concealed, such as underneath a cushion. Cut away any frayed edges around the hole and place the patch in position: from the back on a loose cover, or by tucking it through the hole in a fixed one. Spread fabric adhesive carefully, both on the top edges of the patch and the underside of the fabric around the hole. Wait for the adhesive to become tacky, then press the two surfaces together, taking care to eliminate wrinkles.

impossible to remove, and this will weaken the fibres.

Remove spills immediately, then use a spot-remover to treat stains, but remember to check that the product is suitable for the fabric involved, and test first for colour. Using a white cloth and small circular movements, work gently toward the centre of the stain, taking care not to over-wet your upholstery. Where large areas of a fitted cover have become badly soiled, an upholstery shampoo may be needed. Again, you should avoid excess wetness, so try a dry shampoo, which comes out of the applicator as foam, then dries to a powder that can be vacuumed away.

If you have a lot of upholstered furniture that needs cleaning, you can hire a firm of specialists to come into your home with a large soil extraction machine of the type that is used for carpets. Treat stains with a spot remover first for best results.

It is usually recommended that loose covers are dry cleaned, but many fabrics will respond well to careful washing if you ascertain their fibre content and treat them accordingly. Use warm water and liquid detergent (or make sure the powder is completely dissolved), squeeze or spin, then iron large flat sections and any frilled or pleated valance. Replace the cover while it is still slightly damp so it can be stretched gently into place; if you wait until it dries completely, it may have shrunk slightly and be difficult to fit, while if it dries *in situ*, it will shrink taut over the frame. Covers for awkwardly-shaped chairs can be ironed in position.

INDEX

Acknowledgments

Illustrators: Mulkern Rutherford Studio; pages 38-9 Diane Tippell.

The publisher thanks the following photographers and organizations for their kind permission to reproduce the photographs in this book:

Abitare (Ornella Sancassani) 9 (Cesare Colombo) 46-47 (Gabriele Basilico) 72-73; Camera Press 16-17, 17 below, 25, 32, 47 below, 64-65, 67; Gilles de Chabaneix 58 (Agnes Comar) 23 above; Good Housekeeping (David Brittain) 54 (Ken Kirkwood) 56-57; Habitat 8-9, 59, 61; La Maison de Marie Claire (Rozès/Hirsch-Marie) 6-7 (McLean/Berthier) 14-15 (Nico Dhar/MP Pellé) 16 (Dirand/N Chauvel) 17 above (Hussenot/Charras) 43 left (Chabaneix/Puech) 43 right (Pataut/Bayle) 47 above, 63, 75, 77 (Pataut/Puech) 55 left (Eriaud/Comte) 55 right, 74 above (Chabaneix/Comte) 60 (Chabaneix/Bayle) 72 (G Mahe/M Mahe) 74 below; Marie Claire (Korniloff/Olny) 44-45; Bill McLaughlin 34-35, 36-37; Bent Rej 40-41; Fritz von der Schulenberg 23 below; Elizabeth Whiting & Associates 51 (Michael Dunne) 2, 10-11, 12, 13 (Tim Street-Porter) 33, 50, 65 (Spike Powell) 42 (Michael Nicholson) 45 (Neil Lorimer) 49 (David Cripps) 53 (Tom Leighton) 69.

The following photographs were taken especially for Conran Octopus:

John Heseltine 19, 26, 27, 30; Shona Wood 28-29.